De/constructing Literacies

This book is part of the Peter Lang Education list.
Every volume is peer reviewed and meets
the highest quality standards for content and production.

PETER LANG
New York • Bern • Berlin
Brussels • Vienna • Oxford • Warsaw

Amélie Lemieux

De/constructing Literacies

Considerations for Engagement

PETER LANG
New York • Bern • Berlin
Brussels • Vienna • Oxford • Warsaw

Library of Congress Cataloging-in-Publication Data

Names: Lemieux, Amélie, author.
Title: De/constructing literacies: considerations for engagement /
Amélie Lemieux.
Description: New York: Peter Lang Publishing, 2020.
Includes bibliographical references and index.
Identifiers: LCCN 2019030771 | ISBN 978-1-4331-7282-3 (hardback: alk. paper)
ISBN 978-1-4331-7283-0 (paperback: alk. paper) | ISBN 978-1-4331-5609-0 (ebook pdf)
ISBN 978-1-4331-5610-6 (epub) | ISBN 978-1-4331-5611-3 (mobi)
Subjects: LCSH: Literacy—Study and teaching. | Language arts. |
Reading. | Knowledge, Theory of.
Classification: LCC LC149.L373 2020 | DDC 418/.4—dc23
LC record available at https://lccn.loc.gov/2019030771
DOI 10.3726/b13448

Bibliographic information published by **Die Deutsche Nationalbibliothek.**
Die Deutsche Nationalbibliothek lists this publication in the "Deutsche Nationalbibliografie"; detailed bibliographic data are available on the Internet at http://dnb.d-nb.de/.

The paper in this book meets the guidelines for permanence and durability of the Committee on Production Guidelines for Book Longevity of the Council of Library Resources.

29 Broadway, 18th floor, New York, NY 10006
www.peterlang.com

Printed in the United States of America

To my immediate and academic families, and to my mother Francine (1948–2009), who brought me to the library weekly from the day I was born. Her legacy lives on.

Table of Contents

Figures

Introduction

The title of this book, *De/constructing Literacies: Considerations for Engagement*, refers to ongoing conversations and debates about the nature of literacies and, more importantly, the relationships between definitions and dimensions of engagement in literacy studies. Under the supervision of Jennifer Rowsell (for postdoctoral training) and Boyd White (for doctoral studies), I studied the epistemological traditions of phenomenological hermeneutics in reception studies, material culture, and more recently multimodal receptions and productions as they relate to such epistemologies as phenomenology, visual culture, new materialism, and posthumanism. This book is a dedication to them as a result of our work together and the provoking conversations that took place over a number of years. In the last few years, the research I have conducted with high school and post-secondary students, as well as with pre- and in-service teachers, speaks to these intricate relationships, and further exemplifies the often-fleeting and oblivious inchoate dimensions embedded in the human, the non-human, and the more-than human. The projects I present in this book are in line with current research focusing on the relationship between youth's intra-actions and affective states within textualities and materialities, specifically as to how they shape literacies in plural and open forms (Dernikos, 2018; Kuby & Rowsell, 2017; Kuby, Spector & Thiel, 2018; Lemieux & Rowsell, 2020; Nichols & Campano, 2017; Sherbine, 2018; Wargo, 2018) and in relation to affective entanglements (Ehret & Rowsell, 2020; Leander & Ehret, 2019).

Posthuman research on literacy practices focuses on decentering, in part, the sole emphasis on students, and reconsiders students as a whole. That is, focusing on their interactions with the world, the objects, the digital, their environment, and their inner and outer circles. Researching with posthumanism (Barad, 2007; Braidotti, 2013; Grosz, 2017) in literacy studies has previously been done with emphasis on: rhizoanalysis and educational studies (Ehret, 2016; Semetsky & Masny, 2013); second-language education and citizenship (Fleming, Waterhouse, Bangou & Bastien, 2017); trauma literatures and sticky, affective entanglements and trauma literacies (Dernikos, 2018); early childhood literacies and methodologies (Kuby, 2017; Kuby & Rowsell, 2017); early childhood play and literacies (Marsh, 2017; Sherbine, 2018); adolescent literacies and affective states (Ehret, 2018; Lewis & Tierney, 2013); sexual cultures and youth digital literacies (Handyside & Ringrose, 2017; Renold & Ringrose, 2017); movement and youth literacies (Hackett & Somerville, 2017; Leander & Rowe, 2006; Nordquist, 2017); classroom makerspaces in preschool settings (Wohlwend, Peppler, Keune & Thompson, 2017); sonic literacies and aural rhetorics (Brownell & Wargo, 2017; Ceraso, 2018); work with exceptional youth (Reddington & Price, 2018); and methodologies in the digital age to look at virtual worlds and big data sets (Savin-Baden & Tombs, 2017).

In their volume on literacy and posthumanism, Kuby, Spector, and Thiel (2018) engage with manuscripts covering four main areas: (1) agency (2) intra-activity and entanglement (3) subjectivity and (4) affect. These four dimensions are pivotal in understanding new directions in literacy studies, especially in looking at more-than-human dimensions and epistemologies of being-with (Lemieux & Rowsell, 2020). The research I present in this book seeks to decentralize traditional literacies insofar as it considers students' intra-actions in response to narratives and their adapted versions. Looking across interviews, questionnaires, maps, student commentary, and ekphrastic poetry, I adopted a phenomenological hermeneutics approach that resonates with such posthuman elements as subjectivity and moments of affect in high school students. This research has theoretical underpinnings that align with phenomenological hermeneutics (Ricoeur, 1981; Van Manen, 2014). I explain those dynamic open relationships later on in this manuscript. This is followed by a reflection on the material and its impact on communities—which is inchoate by nature—that brings about change and enthusiasm for daily hidden literacies (Rowsell & Kendrick, 2013).

There is no such thing as immaculate literacies. In a recent study, Rowsell and colleagues (2018) have shown how children in primary-school settings would rather engage, especially in maker education, in sticky literacies (Wargo, 2017), and pedagogies of dissonance between producing and receiving; meaning that both happen, sometimes simultaneously and sometimes anachronously. By pedagogies of dissonance I mean that it is not often clear for children that they are engaging in actual "literacies work" when they are making, reading, browsing, tinkering, and composing (digital) texts. The logic of trial-and-error is useful in considering how we might think of literacies differently, as an ontological way of becoming accustomed to new worlds and words, shapes, and sounds, and new ontologies altogether. The vibrant need to transcend im/materials worlds (Burnett, Merchant, Pahl & Rowsell, 2014) is becoming more and more visible across both home and school contexts.

In this volume, I focus mainly on these questions: How are phenomenological hermeneutics reinvested in the twenty-first century? What are the relationships between phenomenological hermeneutics, affect, and posthumanist thought? To answer these questions, I provide reflections based on studies conducted in secondary and post-secondary educational contexts, and provide further avenues for investigation in literacy studies that look at reading and composition.

CHAPTER ONE

Literacies as *Engrenages* or How Phenomenological Hermeneutics Impact Literacy Studies

Phenomenological hermeneutics lay the groundwork for flexible and open investigations into the structured and unstructured layers of the self. As we are thinking about communicative behavior in literacy studies—how a reader may communicate affect for example—one may think about the way through which one can communicate their responses to texts. Phenomenological hermeneutics are always relational; they materialize through communicative modes and moments of human reflection that are forged by elements imperceptible to human nature. These elements are more-than-human, im/material, and, more generally, impossible to pinpoint. They defy cause and effect. They repulse correlations and positivists mindsets.

Phenomenological hermeneutics tend to rely on two major strands: lived experience, or Martin Heidegger's *Dasein*; and hermeneutics, mostly investigated by Gadamer (1975). Phenomenology has had important repercussions for literacy studies. As such, Roland Barthes' essay *Death of the Author* (1984) (un) intentionally created the collateral *Birth of the Reader*. One of his most famous texts, Barthes' *Death of the Author* problematized, in times of post-structuralist French philosophy, the central place of a human subject (the author) and replaced it with that of another human subject (the reader). Analyzing the ways in which Honoré de Balzac's *Sarrasine* (1834) could be read (in English or in French), Barthes' essay showed how Balzac's writing could be confused with that of the narrator (Sarrasine), and that representations of women as being overly sensitive for instance, coincided with sexist generalizations that were infamously common in Balzac's era. The figure and related representations of the "Author" have historically been used as hegemonies—Barthes suggested the figure of the "Author-God" should be carefully discarded; that is to say hermeneutical work should not be based on a person (as a historical, canonical entity) but rather on language. Reading and composition are like puzzles, and the only ones who hold the keys to solving these puzzles are readers and composers.

Now, language has had its representational problems as well, and has often been "granted too much power" (Barad, 2018, p. 223). The 1970s, 1980s, 1990s have seen, with the birth of the reader, a shift to emphasis on student-led learning after decades of literature education that Barthes and many others have described (Freire, 1972; Rosenblatt, 1969). Numerous researchers (Galda & Beach, 2001; Karolides, 2013; Lewis, 2000; Sipe, 1999, and many others) ad(a)opted Rosenblatt's transactional theory of reading, and focused on literacy research that contextualized settings for literacy pedagogies.

The mid-1990s saw the advent of the New Literacy Studies and Social Semiotics era, and has been studied mostly through the lens of multimodality (Kress, 2000; Rowsell, 2013; Rowsell, Kress, Pahl & Street, 2018). Rowsell and Collier (2016) provide a thorough review of those changes and shifts in literacies studies over the past 20 years. Most recently, and as stated earlier, the focus on emotions and affect in literacies research (Ehret, 2018) has redirected matters towards non-representational theory. And so, shifts from the author to the text to the reader, are being reconsidered to focus, relationally, on matter rather than form, persons, or language. The entanglements become more relevant than ever. Text is the relational now, as the subsequent chapters will exemplify. This relational dimension oscillates most often between a combination of typed words on a virtual or printed page, and certainly humans have evolved and adapted to these interplays when they make meaning. And of course, meaning-making depends on other things than schooling, language, reading, and writing (Pahl & Rowsell, 2020).

Ricoeur's Legacy and the Implications of the Post-representational in Literacy Research

Like many others, I see Paul Ricoeur as one of the most influential philosophers of the twentieth century. Drawing on H. S. Gadamer, Ricoeur's work is worth discovering in literacy studies, as his theory on philosophical hermeneutics brings together matters of alterity, identity construction, philosophy of the subject, and ipseity. For example, Ricoeur's philosophy of perception allows researchers to witness the necessary relationship between research on engagement and the "subjective dimension" of posthumanism. That is, the subject still exists but is decentralized as a repository of "truth"; the material comes to matter, and the more-than-human becomes as important as humans. This way of viewing literacy futures is based on the relational and dynamism between non-humans, humans, and more-than-humans (Sheridan, Lemieux, Do Nascimento & Arnseth, 2020).

Relationality and Reciprocity in (the) Making: Pathways for Engagement and Beyond

Maker education and conversations on posthumanism have been at the core of literacy research in recent years (Hackett & Somerville, 2017; Kuby & Rowsell, 2017; Leander & Boldt, 2013; Nichols & Campano, 2017; Pahl & Pool, 2018). Most research has pointed to both the reciprocity and the intra-actions that unfold as students develop their thoughts and reflect on them in a non-linear way. Jennifer Rowsell has done significant work in literacy studies and posthumanism (Rowsell & Shillitoe, 2019; Rowsell et al., 2018; Whitty & Rowsell, 2019) and I was fortunate to learn from her work how posthumanist maker mindsets propel researchers, teachers, and students into a world that disrupts production and emphasizes intensities instead. Following that tradition, posthumanism reshapes the ways humanities think about education (Kuby & Rowsell, 2017), and challenges Western concepts such as "reading," "writing," and "literacy" as separate entities. Indigenous knowledge and epistemologies (Smith, Tuck & Yang, 2018; Tuck & Wang, 2012), phematerialisms (Ringrose, Warfield & Zarabadi, 2018), studies on affect and digital matters (Chanteris & Gregory, 2018; Ehret & Rowsell, 2020; Wargo, 2018), and posthuman performativities (Barad, 2003; Pomerantz & Raby, 2018; Ringrose & Rawlings, 2015) exemplify how there needs to be a shift to decentralize Westernized hegemonies. This change needs to deconstruct and reverse metaphorical statements that act as a shield to social justice work (see for example, Eve Tuck and K. Wayne Yang's (2012) article "Decolonization is not a Metaphor" as well as work towards indigenizing education and literacies through creative multidimensional modes and outlets (Doucet, 2018; Smith, Tuck & Yang, 2018; Whitty, 2017)). As Braidotti (2013) mentions: the "Humanities [need] to clarify their own methods and mechanisms of knowledge production" (p. 155). Braidotti (2013) calls for a posthuman theory that does not exclude the human, in the sense that it still considers subjectivity, but also includes the more-than-human, the non-human, and the superhuman, in the sense that it is "anti-individualistic" (p. 101) or anti-egocentric as it considers the "other" and fosters social imagination.

Others have offered more practical definitions of posthumanism, emphasizing different directions. For example, Nayar (2014) described his view on critical posthumanism, in that it

> favours co-evolution, symbiosis, feedback and responses as determining conditions rather than autonomy, competition and self-contained isolation of the human. It sees human experience, modes of perception and even self-affective states as essentially derived from, influenced by and formed by the sensoria of numerous other living beings first, and then coming autopoiesis later. (p. 9)

In addition to Nayar, Elizabeth Grosz (2017) describes an ethical dimension and defines "ontoethics" in her book *The Incorporeal* as "an ethics that addresses not just human life in its interhuman relations, but relations between the human and an entire world, both organic and inorganic" (p. 1). This dimension is crucial in literacy research, alluding to the matter of ethics, morals, and consent by centering and considering the essence of being-with, as well as the nature of human interactions with their environments, and vice versa. The question of ethics is also conveyed by Braidotti (2013), who maintains that "the posthuman knowing subject as a time continuum and a collective assemblage implies a double commitment, on the one hand to processes of change and on the other to a strong ethics of eco-sophical sense of community" (p. 169). Thus, an ethos of cohabitation↔interaction between humans and non-humans takes place, and there is an ethical responsibility inherent to posthuman thought (Braidotti, 2013), which implies a pedagogy of care for, and consciousness of, ethics and environmental well-being. Art and literacy education are no strangers to those values.

Posthumanism unfolds in ways that are unpredictable and unscripted; I present in the next section a contemporary example of this. In a recent visit to my Alma Mater, I took an afternoon to visit Alexander Calder's Fall 2018 exhibit at the Montreal Museum of Fine Arts. I spent some time walking through the showrooms allocated for a recollection of Calder's training and experiences of working as a sheet metals welder and as maker-designer of a miniature-size circus. His meshing of sculptural and painting practices, while not new, shifted the world of architectural design in the mid-twentieth century. Calder's work offers a solid rendering of the hybridity between maker mindsets and the arts. The immersive pathways the museum offered speak to current research on posthumanist thought and museum immersion (MacRae, Hackett, Holmes & Jones, 2017). While I briefly recollect my experiences as a museum visitor, those experiences were rooted in the relational, the 'stickness' that happens between humans, more-than-humans, and the self/ves, speaking to the very fact that "meaning," MacRae and colleagues

(2017) argue, "emerges from diffuse and diverse relationships between non-human and human" (p. 507).

I have been inspired by the propositions put forward by Boyd White (McGill University), Anita Sinner (Concordia University), and Darlene St. Georges (Lethbridge University) in a recent article titled "Interweavings: Threads of Art Education, Poetry, and Phenomenological Grapplings" published in the *Canadian Review of Art Education*. In the article, the authors expand on artful "noematic, or reflexive" (White, Sinner & St. Georges, 2018, p. 32) interweavings and responses to Hari Sawa's airplane multimodal work, meshing together sounds, destinations, and themes like movement, place, space, and being-with im/material (Burnett, Merchant, Pahl & Rowsell, 2014). The following work is a second example of those diffuse relationships and comes from a presentation I gave with White, Sinner and St. Georges building on that article and Sawa's work. In the same fashion as my co-presenters, I produced ekphrastic poetry (Heffernan, 2004; Kennedy, 2013; White, 2014; White & Lemieux, 2015, 2017), which corresponds to a produced, verbal, or written materialization of a visual representation. While posthumanism aims at decentering the Anthropocene and human perspectives, this rendition of a Montreal walk speaks rather to phenomenological hermeneutics (Heidegger, 1962; Ricoeur, 1981). The exercise takes us, through still shots of a particularly cold and whimsical night, into my intra-actions (Braidotti, 2013) as I walk from my old Montreal neighborhood to the Old Port. Some research epistemologies will frame these dimensions as multimodal, others as artful; I welcome both perspectives and see them as non-exclusionary, in the tradition of people who have been influential in my thinking (Barton & Baguley, 2014; Chabanne, Lacelle & Richard, 2017; Pahl & Rowsell, 2010; Pool & Pahl, 2015; Rowsell, 2018; Sameshima, White & Sinner, 2018).

Walking, Traces, and Relational Oscillations of the Once Spoken

Silence in motion, advances in time
While its moving essence dances in our minds
Whose light are you keeping in?
Whose soul are you keeping out?
Ruminations of an honest heart with curious bearings
Often still and more often mobile with my thoughts
Whose traces am I reminiscing, following, and unfollowing?
An idea in the making
More truths negotiating
Stillness evokes silence, yet so does movement
Stillness evokes violence, yet so does movement
A straight path with many swerves as one goes along
My old neighborhood, winter lights,

Figure 1: Montreal snow. Amélie Lemieux.

Figure 2: Iced footprints. Amélie Lemieux.

Crisp snow under my rigid boots
Couple of rocks find a way to nest under my socks
A sense of loss provides more purpose when it is brought to the surface

Crackling the ice on the verses
Nothing in the range of subversive
Rather progressive as I go along
Watch out, don't fall
Salt can help break the ice
And forge your way through as you reminisce your thoughts
Watching the city lights

Figure 3: Café crème. Amélie Lemieux.

Now wet asphalt
Boots grippin' gloves on, eco transportation
Standing still in my mind
Queen, witness of those events
A breakup, a new gig
A collaboration for a science project
A taxi on the corner waiting
New customer, barbershop
Colours
Textures in sounds
Dialects, dialogism
Vibrant minds, earthquake ideas
Shaking the world back and forth at the same time

Figure 4: Wet streets, reflecting lights. Amélie Lemieux.

Vieux-Montréal, café crème long gone
Damp boots now,
thoughts still remain
Still the odour of wet snow marching in March
Wearing gloves,
too humid,
take them off.
Earlier conversations made it to here
Through the metro, the Uber, the last-minute ride
They are here on this colonized land with piercing azure columns
Everything I learned is troubled by these conventions
Patterns, gold squares on the left. Who is working at this hour?
Mind, silence, economy, money
Building presence, empty streets, where learning happens.
Wander through

Look up: dark skies, full moon, cosmopolitan lights
The silence and the ideas that the wind brings about
From one soul to another, who gets to pass and who gets stopped?
Who enters a straight path, the enlightened?
As I wander still
Within these thoughts are
The aesthetics of the night

Figure 5: Lights in line. Amélie Lemieux.

> The sonic features of my mind resonating with others
> Materiality operates as a result
> Of what is silenced
> And what persists to be.

These five moments of poetry, paired with photographs I took as I walked alone in Montreal streets, are dynamic representations of feelings-in-the-moment. Prosser (1998) details the benefit of using photographs to convey more than words can express, and gives considerations to taking photographs as one walks and observes her surroundings,

> Through our use of photographs we can discover and demonstrate relationships that may be subtle or easily overlooked. We can communicate the feeling or suggest the emotion imparted by activities, environments, and interactions. And we can provide a degree of tangible detail, a sense of being there, and a way of knowing that may not readily translate into other symbolic modes of communication (p. 102)

As a literacy researcher who is interested in multimodality and the arts, I am comfortable sharing these representations through language as expressive fictions, all the while recognizing the strong methodological contributions of affect, movement, and embodiment in literacy studies and anthropology (Ehret, 2018). The significance of walking-methodology literacy studies and research brings about reflections of thoughts-in-the-process associated with experiences. For example,

Mills and colleagues (2014) retraced how children emotionally react to situated spaces and places through digital filmmaking. They found that children could use positive language to engage with photographs of playgrounds, and how certain words spoke to embodied practices, feelings, and affective states in response to local places. In a related study, Mills, Comber and Kelly (2013) presented Indigenous and non-Indigenous teenagers' documentations of their interactions with the local, emphasizing senses, bodily mobilizations, presence, situational awareness, and mobilities through filmmaking. Similar practices have been used recently through cellphilming and mobile culture productions and processes, particularly in representations of voices in national and international settings (Dahya, 2017; Dayha & King, 2018; MacEntee, Burkholder & Schwab-Cartas, 2016). Nordquist (2017) further problematized mobile literacies by offering walking renditions of high school students engaging with digital literacies across and within spaces in New York streets and public transit on their way to school, videotaping students' literacy dynamisms and seeing the literacy practices emerge as they are paired with mobilities and immobilities.

In the context of a children's hospital, Ehret (2018) found that his relational entanglements with literacy teaching, as exemplified by fictocritical renderings of his connections with a patient named Cole, were reconstructed through multiple felt means such as conversations, ethnographic notes, and video footage as open methodologies. Walking was an important feature of the research process in Ehret's (2018) study, as epiphanies emerged and forged as he was walking towards the hospital to meet with Cole on multiple occasions. Moving and shifting places thus influence thought processes on the move, as do photographs, snapshots depicting engagements with lived experiences, play, and daily moments. Conveying these moments through photographs "account for the inextricable interrelationships between place and the sensing body" (Mills, Comber & Kelly, 2013, p. 25).

Ekphrasis, as shown in the example above and in the poems written by students throughout this book, can be situated manifestations of these literacies 'on the move' (Hollett, Phillips & Leander, 2017) in the multiple spheres of the world we live in. Research on mobilities and literacies have further reviewed how learning might happen across mobilities and in spaces beyond the classroom, and with human and non-human actors (Leander, Phillips & Taylor, 2010). Pursuing this idea, Taylor (2018) used walking as method to "provide jolts of reappraisal with/in the land that swirl the researcher through layers of historical sedimentation she was previously too busy to see" (p. 2), and looked at how history shaped privileges, and constructed systematic racism and oppression.

And so: walking. Walking is a routine activity most people use to get somewhere, exercise, move towards or away from, and live. For me, most of my thinking happens when I walk, and during that activity my thoughts are fleeting, rhizomatic, and dynamic; I cannot get them on paper. Reminders, navigations, memories, anxieties, flows, (de)attachments to the (im)material, felt grounds, troubleshooting, and problem-solving: the vibrations and flux that walking provokes in my head cannot be seized in a sentence. In a study detailing intra-activity at the dynamic intersections of Indigenous oral storytelling, mindful walking, and making a wood canoe, Honeyford (2015) expressed how walking not only allows the researcher to pause and reflect, or to engage in "cautious attention", but also to notice, like Taylor (2018), what is typically unseen. Adopting a posthuman approach and building on Barad (2007), Honeyford writes: "in the threshold, I become both de-centered and centered, part of the larger forces of the world around me; their movement and becoming part of my own" (Honeyford, 2015, p. 216). Martin Buber's (1958) *I-thou* philosophy illustrates those relationships within the self and with the world, emphasizing relational and embodied experiences, which are inherent to the human and more-than-human conditions.

Mapping Literacies: Pathways for Engagement

As such, the act of mapping surfaces the intensities of reading as an immanent practice and develops a rhizomatic cartography for it, and also engages and positions the self as an ontological subject in the world. Additionally, as readers get immersed in a narrative, they will most likely see elements that either differ from their experiences or resemble them: "it is primarily through my engagement with what is not me that I effect the integration of my senses, and thereby experience my own unity and coherence" (Abram, 1996, p. 125).

Mapping the Place of Objects: Accessible Literacies and the Little Free Library (LFL) Project

According to posthuman thought, and as we saw in this introduction, objects exercise relational power. They do so in different ways than humans, but they shape the ways human see and enact in real time. They contextualize conversations on matter (Barad, 2018). Like Taylor (2018), I engaged in a reflexive practice while walking through the hallways of McGill University; I noticed an affluence of printed books resting on benches. People would be walking from one classroom to another, rushing from one office to the next, and normally we would find those books as part of the décor. Some of us would browse on occasion or pick them up for good use when they were relevant. I had already noticed little free library hubs in my neighborhood where people (mostly children) could take, donate, or exchange books. I adapted this concept in a pilot project I co-launched with one of my colleagues in the Faculty of Education at McGill. The initial phase consisted in sourcing sustainable and recyclable materials and put together the first LFL at McGill. The community-at-large—students, staff, faculty, parents, guests—highly benefited from the initiative, which revitalized literacies in that particular academic setting (Lemieux & McLarnon, 2018). Given this appraisal and several recognitions for that project (Quebec Lieutenant Governor's Medal for Community Engagement; McGill University Community Engagement Award), I co-lead phase 2 of the project with the financial support of McGill's Sustainable Projects Fund, whose mission is to develop sustainability futures on campus through the implementation of interdisciplinary projects. One of the main goals of the fund is to further "empower individuals to be the change agents in their own studying and working environment" (McGill Sustainability Projects Fund webpage), which meant it was an ideal venue to expand the LFL concept to other faculties and buildings. With a keen interest in literacy and sustainability, Merika Ramundo, Communications Director at McGill University, Elena Bouton, a Berkeley graduate colleague, and I partnered to expand the project to five campus locations. In the final chapter of this book, I share a theoretical perspective on the transition from the pilot project to its full expansion (18 locations at the moment) and expertise for those educators, literacy experts and enthusiasts, and researchers wanting to replicate this project in their respective post-secondary communities.

References

Abram, D. (1996). *The spell of the sensuous: Perception and language in a more-than-human world.* New York, NY: Vintage Books.

Barad, K. (2003). Posthuman performativity: Toward an understanding of how matter comes to matter. *Signs: Journal of Women in Culture and Society, 28*(3), 801–831.

Barad, K. (2007). *Meeting the universe halfway: Quantum physics and the entanglement of matter and meaning.* Durham, NC: Duke University Press.

Barad, K. (2018). Posthumanist performativity: Toward an understanding of how matter comes to matter. In C. Åsberg & R. Braidotti (Eds.), *A feminist companion to the posthumanities* (pp. 223–239). Cham, Switzerland: Springer.

Barthes, R. (1984). La mort de l'auteur. In R. Barthes, *Essais critiques IV : Le bruissement de la langue* (pp. 63–69). Paris, France: Seuil.

Barton, G. & Baguley, M. (2014). Learning through story: A collaborative multimodal arts approach. *English Teaching: Practice and Critique, 13*(2), 93–112.

Braidotti, R. (2013). *The posthuman*. Malden, MA: Polity.

Brownell, C. J. & Wargo, J. M. (2017). (Re)educating the senses to community literacies: Prospective teachers using sonic cartography to listen for culture. *Multicultural Education Review*, 9(3), 201–214.

Buber, M. (1958). *I and Thou*. New York, NY: Scribner.

Burnett, C., Merchant, G., Pahl, K. & Rowsell, J. (2014). The (im)materiality of literacy: The significance of subjectivity to new literacies research. *Discourse: Studies in the Cultural Politics of Education*, *35*(1), 90–103.

Ceraso, S. (2018). *Sounding composition: Multimodal pedagogies for embodied listening*. Pittsburgh, PA: University of Pittsburgh Press.

Chabanne, J.-C., Lacelle, N. & Richard, M. (Eds.). (2017). Relations intersémiotiques en didactiques des arts et de la littérature [Special issue]. *Revue de recherches en littératie médiatique multimodale, 6*.

Charteris, J. & Gregory, S. (2018). Snapchat and digitally mediated sexualised communication: Ruptures in the school home nexus. *Gender and Education*. doi: 10.1080/09540253.2018.1533922

Dahya, N. (2017). Critical perspectives on youth digital media production: 'Voice' and representation in educational contexts. *Learning, Media and Technology*, *42*(1), 100–111.

Dahya, N. & King, W. E. (2018). Feminist perspectives and mobile culture(s): Power and participation in girls' digital video making communities. In L. S. Berliner & R. Krabill (Eds.), *Feminist interventions in participatory media* (pp. 34–42). New York, NY: Routledge.

Dernikos, B. P. (2018). 'It's like you don't want to read it again': Exploring affects, trauma and 'willful' literacies. *Journal of Early Childhood Literacy*. doi: 10.1177/1468798418756187

Doucet, A. (2018, January). Decolonizing family photographs: Ecological imaginaries and non-representational ethnographies. *Journal of Contemporary Ethnography*, 1–29.

Ehret, C. (2016). Mapping place, affect, and futures in an adolescent's new media making: Schizoanalytic cartographies. In R. Parry, C. Burnett & G. Merchant (Eds.), *Literacy, media, technology: Past, present and future* (pp. 93–108). London, England: Bloomsbury.

Ehret, C. (2018). Moments of teaching and learning in a children's hospital: Affects, textures, and temporalities. *Anthropology & Education Quarterly*, *49*(1), 53–71.

Ehret, C. & Rowsell, J. (2020). Special issue: Affect and educational studies. *Reading Research Quarterly*.

Fleming, D., Waterhouse, M., Bangou, F. & Bastien, M. (2017). Agencement, second language education and becoming: A Deleuzian take on citizenship. *Critical Inquiry in Language Studies*, *15*(2), 141–160. doi: 10.1080/15427587.2017.1365237

Freire, P. (1972). *Pedagogy of the oppressed*. New York, NY: Herder and Herder.

Gadamer, H.-G. (1975). *Truth and method*. New York, NY: Seabury Press.

Galda, L. & Beach, R. (2001). Response to literature as a cultural activity. *Reading Research Quarterly*, *36*(1), 64–73.

Grosz, E. (2017). *The incorporeal: Ontology, ethics, and the limits of materialism*. New York, NY: Columbia University Press.

Hackett, A. & Somerville, M. (2017). Posthuman literacies: Young children moving in time, place and more-than-human worlds. *Journal of Early Childhood Literacy*, *17*(3), 374–391.

Handyside, S. & Ringrose, J. (2017). Snapchat memory and youth digital sexual cultures: Mediated temporality, duration and affect. *Journal of Gender Studies*, *26*(3), 347–360.

Heffernan, J. A. (2004). *Museum of words: The poetics of ekphrasis from Homer to Ashbery*. Chicago, IL: University of Chicago Press.

Heidegger, M. (1962). *Being and time*. London, England: SCM Press.

Hollett, T., Phillips, N. C. & Leander, K. M. (2017). Digital geographies. In K. A. Mills, A. Stornaiuolo, A. Smith & J. Zacher Pandya (Eds.), *Routledge handbook of writing, literacies, and education in digital cultures*. New York, NY: Routledge.

Honeyford, M. (2015). Thresholds of possibility—mindful walking, traditional oral storytelling, and the birch bark canoe: Theorizing material intra-activity in an afterschool arts space. *Literacy Research: Theory, Method, and Practice*, *64*, 210–226.

Karolides, N. J. (2013). *Reader response in secondary and college classrooms*. New York, NY: Routledge.

Kennedy, D. (2013). *The ekphrastic encounter in contemporary British poetry and elsewhere*. Farnham, England: Ashgate.

Kress, G. (2000). Multimodality. In B. Cope & M. Kalantzis (Eds.), *Multiliteracies: Literacy learning and the design of social futures* (pp. 182–202). London, England: Routledge.

Kuby, C. R. (2017). Poststructural and posthuman theories as literacy research methodologies: Tensions and possibilities. In R. Zaidi & J. Rowsell (Eds.), *Literacy lives in transcultural times* (pp. 157–174). New York, NY: Routledge.

Kuby, C. R. & Rowsell, J. (2017). Early literacy and the posthuman: Pedagogies and methodologies. *Journal of Early Childhood Literacy*, *17*(3), 285–296.

Kuby, C. R., Spector, K. & Thiel, J. (2018). *Posthumanism and literacy education: Knowing/becoming/doing literacies*. New York, NY: Routledge.

Leander, K. M. & Boldt, G. M. (2013). Rereading "A pedagogy of multiliteracies": Bodies, texts, and emergence. *Journal of Literacy Research*, *45*(1), 22–46.

Leander, K. M. & Ehret, C. (Eds.). (2019). *Affect in literacy teaching and learning: Pedagogies, politics, and coming to know*. New York, NY: Routledge.

Leander, K. M., Phillips, N. C. & Taylor, K. H. (2010). The changing social spaces of learning: Mapping new mobilities. *Review of Research in Education*, *34*, 329–394.

Leander, K. M. & Rowe, D. W. (2006). Mapping literacy spaces in motion: A rhizomatic analysis of a classroom literacy performance. *Reading Research Quarterly*, *41*, 428–460. doi: 10.1598/RRQ.41.4.2

Lemieux, A. & McLarnon, M. (2018). Artful portable library spaces: Increasing community agency and shared knowledge. In E. Hasebe-Ludt & C. Leggo (Eds.), *Canadian curriculum studies: A Métissage of inspiration/imagination/interconnection* (pp. 35–46). Toronto, ON: Canadian Scholars' Press.

Lemieux, A. & Rowsell, J. (2020). Taking a wide-angled view of contemporary digital literacy. In O. Erstad, R. Flewitt, B. Kümmerling-Meibauer & Í. S. Pires Pereira (Eds.), *The Routledge handbook of digital literacies in early childhood* (pp. 453–463). New York: Routledge.

Lewis, C. (2000). Critical issues: Limits of identification: The personal, pleasurable, and critical in reader response. *Journal of Literacy Research, 32*(2), 253–266.

Lewis, C. & Tierney, J. D. (2013). Mobilizing emotion in an urban classroom: Producing identities and transforming signs in a race-related discussion. *Linguistics and Education, 23*, 289–304.

MacEntee, K., Burkholder, C. & Schwab-Cartas, J. (Eds.). (2016). *What's a cellphilm?: Integrating mobile phone technology into participatory arts based research and activism.* Rotterdam, Netherlands: Sense Publishers.

MacRae, C., Hackett, A., Holmes, R. & Jones, L. (2017). Vibrancy, repetition and movement: Posthuman theories for reconceptualising young children in museums. *Children's Geographies, 16*(5), 503–515.

Marsh, J. A. (2017). The internet of toys: A posthuman and multimodal analysis of connected play. *Teachers College Record, 119*, Art. No. 120305. ISSN 0161-4681

Mills, K. A., Comber, B. & Kelly, P. (2013). Sensing place: Embodiment, sensoriality, kinesis, and children behind the camera. *English Teaching: Practice and Critique, 12*(2), 11–27.

Mills, K. A., Unsworth, L., Bellochi, A., Park J. Y. & Ritchie, S. (2014). Children's emotions and multimodal appraisal of places: Walking with the camera. *Australian Journal of Language and Literacy, 37*(3), 171–181.

Nayar, P. K. (2014). *Posthumanism.* Cambridge, England: Polity.

Nichols, T. P. & Campano, G. (2017). Post-humanism and literacy studies. *Language Arts, 94*(4), 245–251.

Nordquist, B. (2017). *Literacy and mobility.* New York, NY: Routledge.

Pahl, K. & Pool, S. (2018). Re-imagining artistic subjectivities within community projects. *Open Library of Humanities, 4*(2), 2. doi: 10.16995/olh.248

Pahl, K. & Rowsell, J. (2010). *Artifactual literacies: Every object tells a story.* New York, NY: Teachers College Press.

Pahl, K. & Rowsell, J. with Collier, D., Pool, S., Rasool, Z., & Trzecak, T. (2020). Living literacies. Boston, MA: MIT Press.

Pomeranz, S. & Raby, R. (2018). Bodies, hoodies, and success: Post-human performativity and smart girlhood. *Gender and Education.* doi: 10.1080/09540253.2018.1533923

Pool, S. & Pahl, K. (2015). The work of art in the age of mechanical co-production. In D. O'Brien & P. Matthews (Eds.), *After urban regeneration: Communities, policy and place* (pp. 79–94). Bristol, England: Bristol University Press.

Prosser, J. (Ed.). (1998). *Image-based research: A sourcebook for qualitative researchers.* London, England: Falmer.

Reddington, S. & Price, D. (2018). Pedagogy of new materialism: Advancing the educational inclusion agenda for children and youth with disabilities. *Disability Studies Quarterly, 38*(1). Retrieved from http://dsq-sds.org/article/view/5945/4879

Renold, E. & Ringrose, J. (2017). Selfies, relfies and phallic tagging: Posthuman participations in teen digital sexuality assemblages. *Education, Philosophy and Theory, 49*, 1066–1079. doi: 10.1080/00131857.2016.1185686

Ricoeur, P. (1981). *Hermeneutics and the human sciences: Essays on language, action and interpretation* (J. Thompson, Trans.). Cambridge, MA: Cambridge University Press, and Paris, France: Éditions de la Maison des Sciences de l'Homme.

Ricoeur, P. (1992). *Oneself as another*. Chicago, IL: Chicago University Press.

Ringrose, J. & Rawlings, V. (2015). Posthuman performativity, gender and 'school bullying': Exploring the material-discursive intra-actions of skirts, hair, sluts, and poofs. *Confero, 3*(2), 1–37.

Ringrose, J., Warfield, K. & Zarabadi, S. (Eds.). (2018). *Feminist posthumanisms: New materialisms and education*. New York, NY: Routledge.

Rosenblatt, L. M. (1969). Towards a transactional theory of reading. *Journal of Literacy Research, 1*(1), 31–49.

Rowsell, J. (2013). *Working with multimodality: Rethinking literacy in a digital age*. London, England: Routledge.

Rowsell, J. (Ed.). (2018). *The art and craft of literacy pedagogy: Profiling community arts zone*. New York, NY: Routledge.

Rowsell, J. & Collier, D. (2016). Researching multimodality in language and education. In K. King, Y.-J. Lai & S. May (Eds.), *Research methods in language and education, encyclopedia of language and education* (3rd ed.). Cham, Switzerland: Springer.

Rowsell, J. & Kendrick, M. (2013). Boys' hidden literacies: The critical need for the visual. *Journal of Adolescent and Adult Literacy, 56*(7), 587–599.

Rowsell, J., Kress, G., Pahl, K. & Street, B. V. (2018). The social practice of multimodal reading: A New Literacy Studies-Multimodal perspective on reading. In D. E. Alvermann, N. J. Unrau, M. Sailors & R. B. Ruddell (Eds.), *Theoretical models and processes of literacy* (7th ed.). New York, NY: Routledge.

Rowsell, J., Lemieux, A., Swartz, L., Burkitt, J. & Turcotte, M. (2018). The stuff that heroes are made of: Elastic, sticky, messy literacies in children's transmedial cultures. *Language Arts, 96*(1), 7–20.

Rowsell, J. & Shillitoe, M. (2019). The craftivists: Pushing for affective, materially informed pedagogy. *British Journal of Educational Technology, 50*(4), 1544–1559.

Sameshima, P., White, B. & Sinner, A. (Eds.). (2018). *MA: Materiality in teaching and learning*. New York, NY: Peter Lang.

Savin-Baden, M. & Tombs, G. (2017). *Research methods in education for the digital age*. London, England: Bloomsbury.

Semetsky, I. & Masny, D. (2013). *Deleuze and education*. Edinburgh, England: Edinburgh University Press.

Sherbine, K. (2018). Track Star + thing power: Be(com)ing in the literacy workshop. *Journal of Early Childhood Literacy*. doi: 10.1177/1468798418777847

Sheridan, M. P., Lemieux, A., Do Nascimento, A. & Arnseth, H. C. (2020). Intra-active entanglements: What posthuman and new materialist frameworks can offer the learning sciences. *British Journal of Educational Technology*. doi: 10.1111/1467-8535.12928

Sipe, L. R. (1999). Children's response to literature: Author, text, reader, context. *Theory into Practice*, *38*(3), 120–129.

Smith, L., Tuck, E. & Yang, K. (2018). *Indigenous and decolonizing studies in education: Mapping the long view*. New York, NY: Routledge.

Taylor, K. H. (2018). The role of public education in place-remaking: From a retrospective walk through my hometown to a call to action. *Cognition and Instruction*. doi: 10.1080/07370008.2018.1460844

Tuck, E. & Wayne Yang, K. (2012). Decolonization is not a metaphor [online]. *Decolonization: Indigeneity, Education & Society*, *1*(1).

Van Manen, M. (2014). *Phenomenology of practice: Meaning-giving methods in phenomenological research and writing*. Walnut Creek, CA: Left Coast Press.

Wargo, J. M. (2017). Rhythmic rituals and emergent listening: Intra-activity, sonic sounds and digital composing with young children. *Journal of Early Childhood Literacy, 17*(3), 392–408.

Wargo, J. M. (2018). Writing with wearables? Young children's intra-active authoring and the sounds of emplaced invention [online first]. *Journal of Literacy Research*, 1–22.

White, B. (2014). Student generated art criticism. *The Canadian Review of Art Education*, *41*(1), 32–55.

White, B. & Lemieux, A. (2015). Reflecting selves: Pre-service teacher identity development explored through material culture. *Learning Landscapes*, *9*(1), 267–283.

White, B. & Lemieux, A. (2017). *Mapping holistic learning: An introductory guide to aesthetigrams*. New York, NY: Peter Lang.

White, B., Sinner, A. & St. Georges, D. (2018). Interweavings: Threads of art education, poetry, and phenomenological grapplings. *Canadian Review of Art Education*, *45*(1), 32–49.

Whitty, P. (2017). Complicating literacies: Settler ways of being with story(ies) on Wabanaki lands. In R. Zaidi & J. Rowsell (Eds.), *Literacy lives in transcultural times* (Expanding Literacies in Education Series, pp. 17–31). New York, NY: Routledge.

Whitty, P. & Rowsell, J. (2019). Reflective conversations about research methods with children. In N. Kucirkova, J. Rowsell & G. Falloon (Eds.), *The Routledge handbook of learning with technology in early childhood* (pp. 18–29). New York: Routledge.

Wohlwend, K. E., Peppler, K. A., Keune, A. & Thompson, N. (2017). Making sense and nonsense: Comparing mediated discourse and agential realist approaches to materiality in a preschool makerspace. *Journal of Early Childhood Literacy*, *17*(3), 444–462.

CHAPTER TWO

De/constructing Reading Engagement

"Ce que le texte offre, ce sont des schémas pour guider l'imaginaire du lecteur[1]"
—Paul Ricoeur (1985, p. 306)

Reading engagement has had a long tradition of being defined as a fixed entity: an element to be evaluated within classroom walls through standardized testing. While there has been important progress in developing readers' attainment and reading comprehension—mostly in quantitative positivist research settings (see, for example, the long and important legacy of Guthrie, Cox, Metsala, and Wigfield, among others)—there is a need in the literature to address reading engagement as a qualitative component of its own, taking into consideration students' emotions and affective states (Ivey & Johnston, 2018; Lysaker & Miller, 2012). To provide an extensive understanding of reading engagement, in this chapter, I begin by providing an overview of the term "engagement" as used in a recent report conducted by researchers at the University of Alberta. I then review alternative definitions of reading engagement, and explain the research traditions under which they fall. After this, I provide extensive definitions from the literature on "reading motivation" and "interest in reading," and show how these definitions differ from or

1. This citation translates as: "The text offers images to guide the reader's imagination" (my translation).

resemble one another in order to clarify the often vague language around reading engagement. Finally, reflecting on these notions, I present an alternative conceptualization of reading engagement that is substantially oriented towards the inclusion of aesthetic interactions with texts. The discussion is conceptual and terminological. I must clarify that I use the term "text" as an ensemble of multimodal components, and its nature encompasses all types of modalities that are inclusive rather than exclusive (Rowsell, 2013).

Based at the University of Alberta, Parsons and Taylor (2011) explain that the term "engagement" is difficult to summarize within an umbrella term because there are so many categories of engagement to consider (e.g., academic, cognitive, emotional, behavioral, intellectual, institutional, and so on). In their review of the literature, the authors note four dimensions and goals of engagement:

1. when it is linked with achievement and ultimately graduation is the goal;
2. when compliance is the goal, either by complying with the teacher's expectations for behavior and learning objectives or with the students' sense of control over their learning;
3. when the goal is to reach flow experiences (a concept extensively developed by Csikszentmihalyi, 1990); and
4. when the goal is to build improved cognitive and learning skills.

It is my understanding that use of the term "engagement" mostly falls somewhere within the second and third categories, as students' experiences when they interact with texts largely depends on a balance between aesthetic and efferent reading (Rosenblatt, 1978), and students' "sense of control" over the projects they undertake. The scope of engagement extends those parameters, as I will explain below; nonetheless, they provide a basis for discussion on the nature of engagement.

Engagement as a Feature of Social Imagination and Empathy

The links between aesthetic experiences and flow have previously been outlined by White (2007), who explained that Csikszentmihalyi's four categories of aesthetic experience (the sensory, the cognitive, the transcendent and the emotional) are intrinsically linked to feelings that develop empathy and provide an increased sense of self. As Pahl (2014) suggests, the aesthetic dimension plays a significant role in literacy studies, and the felt receptions play an important role in this dimension.

In philosophy of education, significant work has been done to demonstrate that imagination is a condition for empathy development (Greene, 1995), and that a care for others is necessary in order to engage meaningfully with the world.

One key way to develop empathy is through multimodal approaches, and since the mid-1990s, access to these technologies has drastically improved. For example, in 1998, only 26.2% of U.S. households accessed the Internet through a computer at home[2], compared to 2018, when 95% of the US population owned a cellphone—essentially a pocket-sized computer—77% of which were smartphones[3]. With any change comes an ontological, Darwinian adaptation: we have evolved with digital technologies and they, reciprocally, and in a posthuman way, have evolved with us. We can no longer think that print materials are the only material modes to be integrated in classroom settings—doing so would be antithetical to the demographics and to daily life in the US and Canada (Lemieux & Rowsell, 2019).

I would argue, however, that empathy and social imagination are still needed in literacy education, and that there are ways to understand Rosenblatt and Greene's theories of the transactional theory of reading and the social imagination respectively in order to grasp the textured essence of engagement in today's classrooms. Social imagination, defined as the "capacity to invent visions of what should be and what might be" (Greene, 1995, p. 5), is certainly still relevant to today's educational system. If, as researchers and teachers, we adopt dynamic ways of "being/doing/knowing" (Kuby & Rowsell, 2017, p. 285) in the world, and promote and embody dialogues of 'otherness,' then the educational landscape has the potential to nurture not only "citizens of the world" (Nussbaum, 1998), but also coders, makers, gamers, digital readers, and composers of the world. It is within these dimensions that empathy emerges as we conceive and care for potential audiences, transfer passions in digital and online worlds, lose all sense of time as we progress into a multimodal (aural, visual, kinesthetic, sensorial) reception or production. The reception of works—whether monomodal, augmented, or multimodal—creates new worlds of fiction that pertain to the (multimodal) reader. As Ricoeur (1990) notes, "reading, as a space where the world of the narrative transfers—and also the world of literary characters—to that of the reader's world, is a privileged space and relationship to the reading subject"[4] (p. 381). If we contextualize Ricoeur's

2. *Source:* U.S. Department of Commerce, National Telecommunications and Information Administration, *Falling Through the Net: Defining the Digital Divide,* July 1999, *A Nation Online,* 2004, and Economics and Statistics Administration, 2010.
3. Source: Pew Research Centre, http://www.pewinternet.org/fact-sheet/mobile/
4. My English translation of: "La lecture, en tant que milieu où s'opère le transfert du monde du récit – et donc aussi du monde des personnages littéraires – au monde du lecteur, constitue un lieu et un lien privilégiés d'affection au sujet lisant" (p. 381).

thought in today's educational setting, I argue that this narrative transfer can happen through digital contexts in the classroom as well. To illustrate, a student might engage in coding literacies as a way to express her relationships with the characters and ideas she wants to create using software. If we shape "coding as a playground" (Bers, 2018), student coders may have a playful ability to develop their social imagination through stimulating computational thinking in digital spaces (e.g., coding), a process through which learning and producing may take place.

Like any moral value, empathy is manifested at many levels. That is, empathy progresses over many phases (Zahavi, 2016). First, there is the perception of others' expressive states. Second, the one perceiving the other's feeling can "carry out" and undergo the other's experience. Lastly, there is a manifestation of that received perception, and I would argue that progression proceeds from one's ability to express it through such means as the arts, literacy, meditation, and verbal communication.

At the University of Toulouse in Southern France, the empirical work of Gérard Langlade (2013) has shown over the years that there is an inherent need for teachers and educators to consider dimensions in reading such as malaise and surprise to measure a student's engagement qualitatively. For example, a reader discovering the development of a character might find that a particular action or thought (as narrated) makes them feel uncomfortable, uncertain, hesitant, or disturbed. These intra-actions (Barad, 2007), which permeate corporeality and non-corporeality, have the power to dictate what engagement is and what it means for reading research in all its forms (monomodal or multimodal). That is, the reader's malaise can manifest at any moment and in response to any word, thought, or combination of ideas conveyed through monomodal and multimodal platforms. Feelings of malaise and surprise should be welcomed in the classroom, and ideally discussed with peers and instructors to embrace diverse affective perspectives. We will see in subsequent chapters how malaise and surprise can be mobilized as embodied, rhizomatic feelings, and how these can be recorded in mapping strategies like aesthetigrams, concept maps, and open user-generated cartographies. What is important to take away from this conceptualization of reading engagement is that no affective states are to be marginalized, ignored, or left behind; they all contribute to different levels and dimensions of engagement.

I have been very interested lately in understanding "the shape of our thoughts" (Sousanis, 2015) and how that might play a role in research on engagement. I wonder about epistemological questions—how we process and see concepts or, as I like to say, how we 'digest' them. How do we go about being aware of the way we communicate our engagements, if and when do we do so, in situated contexts?

For example, at what point does a student become engaged in a task, and what are the 'shaping' conditions and thoughts that allow for such involvement? Is there a turning point where a student becomes engaged in reading a multimodal text, and if so, what is that point? Within a reading transaction, Rosenblatt (1978) would suggest, a sufficient amount of aesthetic experiences are responsible for reading engagement, and those aesthetic experiences are bendable, perceptual, contextual, and relative. As Eaton and Moore (2002) explain, aesthetic experiences vary, all the while allowing for a certain level of meaning:

> aesthetic experience is a *sorites* phenomenon in that it comes into being when a number of contributory elements add up to a sufficient sum [...] of pertinent traits before we cross a decision line that may be indistinct to us, but in the final analysis makes sense (pp. 16–17).

In a classroom setting that focuses on cultivating aesthetic experiences (such as through participatory video-making or map-making as response to a reading of a novel, for instance) a *sorites* phenomenon alludes to an impossibility in predicting how individual moments of experience may complement each other, in such a way as to culminate in "an" aesthetic experience. That is, aesthetic experiences are cumulative rather than exclusive with regards to meaning: "the meaning of the work is not the same for everyone ... [there are] multiple readings of one work and no reasonable way of saying that one is better than the other" (Parsons, 2002, p. 34). Again, meaning derived from a text is not primarily text-oriented; it depends on various perspectives and contextualities that derive from aesthetic experiences.

To cultivate these aesthetic experiences means breeding the conditions for reading engagement through reception, regardless of the mode of the reading and response. To foster such a culture is to render valuable the idea of sharing perceptions of, and responses to, multimodal narratives in the classroom. Awareness that such possibilities even exist is, of course, crucial in that endeavor. To adopt such a mindset means to shamelessly advocate for the diversity of transactions that need to be explored, as they are the starting point of rich discussions on meaning and values triggered by (or found in) multimodal texts.

In recent years as a researcher, high school teacher, and professor (albeit a new one), I have used such a framework, and it is my hope that you will find in this book a few ideas or glimpses of discussions that interest you as a researcher or educator. What becomes clear, in literacy research and praxis, is that learning is relational and about relationships—the ones we have with materials and humans—and is also inherently dialogic. Building on that natural tendency toward dialogism allows one to predict the outcomes of what literacy education can be.

Engagement and Reflections on Barthes's Contributions to Meaning-Making

Symbolic meaning draws from a common lexicon of symbols that carry meaning which is trapped, Barthes (1982) would argue, in a "system of destination" (p. 45). This system of destination is ever bendable, open, and shaped by our thoughts, conventions, and beliefs (without discrimination and with the inclusion of commonalities such as humorous remarks and all sorts of additional, rhizomatic information). This systemic concept is what Barthes (1982) frames as the obtuse meaning (or the "third meaning"), which is inherently about gearing a response towards *signifiance* (to use Kristeva's term), or meaning-making without having access to a clear signifier. Barthes uses pictures and photographs of *Ivan the Terrible* to make his case. In reading studies and multimodal work, we have access to a series of signifiers, but these semiotic elements, when in symbiosis, transgress and inform reception and meaning-making. It is through the awareness of what those signs 'do,' individually and collectively, that shape how meaning is transferred and received. With the "third meaning," Barthes was able to give the non-representational and the affective a name. Since then, these dimensions have been taken up in literacy studies and multimodal work (among others, Dernikos, 2018; Ehret, Hollett & Jocius, 2016; Kuby, Spector & Thiel, 2018; Pahl & Rowsell, 2020).

The meaning-making process is idiosyncratic. The obtuse meaning is inclusive, permeable, and non-discriminatory. In the original *L'Obvie et l'Obtus (Essais Critiques III)*, Barthes (1982) writes: "I think that the obtuse meaning carries a certain emotion; stuck in disguise, this emotion is never sticky; it is an emotion that simply identifies what we love, what we want to defend, it is an emotion-value, an evaluation" (p. 51)[5].

The aesthetic character that is fleeting in the obtuse meaning is non-representational *and* affective as it weighs in on perceived receptions of artworks and

5. This segment translates as: "*je crois que le sens obtus porte une certaine émotion; prise dans le déguisement, cette émotion n'est jamais poisseuse; c'est une émotion qui désigne simplement ce qu'on aime, ce qu'on veut défendre; c'est une émotion-valeur, une évaluation*" (p. 51). The reason I am referring to the original French text, here, is far from being insignificant. Apart from the fact that I have read all of Barthes' work in French, from *Le Plaisir du Texte* to *S/Z*, I am choosing to provide a phenomenological-hermeneutic translation account, and I am drawing on my work and practical experience in Translation Studies (a field in which I obtained a bachelor's degree at McGill University prior to becoming an educational researcher). My reception of Barthes' work is therefore not mediated by a translation, but rather informed by it. That is, at times, I will refer to English versions for clarification. I see this process as part of a reflexive work that I undertake as a scholar, and I find dual language is both non-exclusive and relational in this way.

their embedded symbolism. Barthes (1970) defended a similar position in *S/Z*, as to explain how plural the writing voice is, and thus how one must rely on interpretation—a hermeneutic state—to make meaning in response to a given text (and that text can well be taken in the larger sense, i.e., a multimodal text). And so, while there exists some skepticism about the weight of meaning the obtuse carries (Attridge, 2010), one must realize, as an educational researcher, that such meaning is sometimes at the core of receptions, transactions, and states of being with texts. Similar to a moving kaleidoscope, the obtuse completely opens the field(s) of reception. Those situated-yet-open understandings are always mediated through some form of language, Ricoeur would argue, and that language may well be multimodal in our current decade. If we compared the state of literacies to what it was in 2000, literacies were not as mobile, instantaneous, and pervasive. Cellphones (let us reminisce about the beloved GSM Nokia cellular phone released in September 2000) had a primary function, which was communicating with someone via dial-talk. Fast-forward 20 years, and we have mostly stopped using the expression 'electronic devices,' a term which was overly popular in the first decade of the twenty-first century. Obsolete are *PalmPilots* (Personal Digital Assistants), brick laptops, and brightly colored iMacs. Digital cameras slowly replaced 35 mm photography lenses, with an option to transform captured photos (immaterial) to printed photos (material) and shared photos (socio-immaterial).

In understanding the ethos of literacies and engagement, the conversations on the immaterial (Burnett, 2015; Burnett, Merchant, Pahl & Rowsell, 2014; Rowsell, 2014) in literacy studies brought about the larger scope of what a literacy learner looks, lives, and acts like. That is, a reader is not only a reader, but also a writer, listener, thinker, maker, and player—an overall "multimodal interactor and intra-actor" who engages with literacies in many, if not all, of its forms. I am making another observation on materiality and engagement; there was a time when switching games on a *GameBoy* depended on having access to individual plastic ROM cartridges. Some of these games adopted a Gallery format, giving players the option to move, internally, from one game to another. This format proposed internal shifts in gaming, which were the beginning of mobile literacies as we know them today in smartphones, where literacies are centralized in one interactive, user-friendly menu. Not only does the phone serve as a repository for the connection between the material and the im/material (e.g., facilitating actions with tangible outcomes like booking trips, to engaging in virtual and mobile game worlds like PokémonGO), but it is also the primary hub today for daily, ubiquitous literacies. Some of these games further speak to multimodality as an entry point to social justice matters in education and beyond (Hawreliak & Lemieux, 2020), and more and more we see these matters being slowly addressed in the gaming industry (or at least it is of concern in the field of education).

Merleau-Ponty's *épokhè*, in the phenomenological tradition, precedes the awareness of the separation between subject and object—a phenomenology that is pervasive in our daily engagements with virtual texts through smartphones, for instance. In an educational context, engagement is a state where learning happens as a process as opposed to a situated, ascribable point in time. One mobilizes similar states of engagement when one reads a comic or watches a movie. For example, one might feel surprised as they engage with a character's journey and decide to become allies with character B instead of character C. As one views a film and progresses with the story, there can be multiple changes and upturns in plot development, which might entice the viewer to find out more and solve the narrative. Questions and bets that play on deductions, for instance, can lead to more engagement as one enters narrative storyworlds. In terms of production, students can do restorying activities such as queerbending and racebending narratives (Thomas & Stornaiuolo, 2016) as to see how those receptions can be re-mobilized to provide more diverse and inclusive representations and counternarratives.

On Post-terms and Engagement

In the literacy-research landscape, recent empirical studies have embraced posthumanism (Barad, 2007; Braidotti, 2013; Nayar, 2014) as a way of being-with literacies, in such areas as early childhood education (Hackett & Somerville, 2017; Kuby & Rowsell, 2017) and in K–12 settings (Baroutsis & Woods, 2018; Kuby, Spector & Thiel, 2018). What is important to know about posthumanism is that it propels daily life and literacies as subjects for research, not only focusing on relationality, but also suggesting new dimensions for understanding unpredictability, adaptability, and the common nexus of learning within literacy research and beyond. Most importantly, relationality helps us think about transforming texts in multimodal literacy contexts, transducing narratives across multiple storyworlds and materialities, thereby accounting for affective tangents in learning (Dernikos & Thiel, 2019; Lemieux, 2019; Rowsell et al., 2018; Deprêtre & Duarte, 2019).

In *Death of the Author*, Barthes (1984) made suggestions that echo some dimensions of posthumanism (beyond Deleuze & Guattari's 1991 concept of rhizome) as we use it today in literacy research. The idea of 'presence,' or lack thereof, was central in Barthes' work, at both the metaphorical and the physical levels. Deconstructing Balzac's *Sarrasine*, Barthes questions who the speaker behind the writer or the narrator is, and what frameworks—philosophical or phenomenological—drive the writing. This reflection brings about a feature of the subject, as reader and writer, that is plural and unpredictable. Nonetheless, Barthes answers, writing is responsible for "the destruction of any voice, any origin," as to say that, by writing, the author loses his self and identity, and that this self and identity is instead to be constructed by the reader. The multiplicity of voices and codes, ever present in the act of writing, are to be reinterpreted by weaving in multiple voices; and there lies a type of anti-humanism defined by a negative hermeneutical ethos: no one can arrive at a "true meaning." Divorced from its privileged title, the author becomes secondary; erased.

The materiality of text, as I have explained earlier, comes with a refusal to make meaning-making stop. It is in this sense that there are relationships and links to be made between Barthes' vision and posthumanism. Barthes' focus on the irreducible plural forms and receptions of text made intertextuality a given, and thus: everything becomes text. In decentralizing the human subject and his mind, posthumanism's *raison d'être* is to look at the more-than-human and the ways of being-with (Kuby & Rowsell, 2017) in the world. For engagement in literacy studies, this epistemology contests any type of superiority, that of the text, the author, the reader, and focuses instead on the multidimensional influences of human/non-human/more-than-human interactions and relationships. For example, a person may construct or shape a text, and that same text may construct or shape that person. Desacralizing the text and the author is one of the strands that Barthes and posthumanism have in common; even if Barthes privileged the reader in ways that accounted for multiple meanings built by that reader. The focus on pluralities in the reader and loss of authorial privilege is one of the key components of that *rapprochement*.

Another point in common would be the unpredictable, or the place of "superunknowns" (St. Clair, 2005), which exist at the threshold of any work—research-based or pedagogical—done in literacy studies and educational research. For instance, as one undertakes research on the nature of reading engagement, it is impossible to predict the types of engagement that a student will go through as he reads, and it therefore calls for *superunknowns*, which bring challenges in replicability in educational research (St. Clair, 2005). The unpredictability factor is at the core of uncertainty in research, which is not to say that admitting those factors hinders research projects and methodologies. On the contrary, the more researchers are in tune with their reflexive practices, the closer they will be to "real" teaching and learning, and the more learning they will engage with themselves.

Embracing the possibility of those 'superunknowns' becomes key. The comfort of play between languages and modalities speaks to multiple understandings of structure and meaning. For example, Marcel Duchamp's modern art and frequent play on words or calembours/puns, *Lits et Ratures* (*littérature*: a literal translation for literature in the early twentieth century) for example, give testimony to the debuts of postmodernism, where the rapports with structure and meaning were becoming more playful. Jean-François Lyotard (1984), considered by many to be one of the early fathers of postmodern thought, built on Wittgenstein's (1953) *Philosophical Investigations* and noticed that play on words contains three open dimensions:

1. words are subject to a transaction between gamers (think of Rosenblatt's transactional theory between the reader and the book as to generate meaning-making),
2. language games are bound by 'rules' by which meaning is dictated, and
3. language games contain moves.

A tangible, personal example is one that resurfaces on a daily basis, which is that of the multiple ways to pronounce my first name: Amélie, Amelie, Amelia, amelie, Emily, "ameele" (notice the lack of accents, changes in letters, and missing capital letters). Though the pronunciations are multiple, they refer to the same person—me. The *intent*—and I emphasize the alluded good intent—is to address 'me,' the *signifié* or the signified, which is a structure and a grammar rule in and of itself. By choosing to voice a name, the more generalized intent is to communicate with. To share with. To be in relation with. This is the essence of the language game without its authoritarian figure as I choose to release its perceived negative effect on me. When I get asked about how my name is pronounced, or rather what is the 'best way' to pronounce my name, I understand that most of the time the intent is to find a correct way to engage with my person and represent it orally (*la parole*). The intent does not lie within me; it is external and beyond my control. I choose to let go and assert that any pronunciation is good, and provide a few examples of the ways one can pronounce my name. If someone calls me Amelia, my 'cultural heritage' does not feel threatened, although I can understand why some feel that way. I see my name as a word, one that is malleable. Its practical purpose is for others to communicate with me. I feel fortunate, on the contrary, that a person feels comfortable enough to engage in this discursive relationship. Those types of feelings and affective states associated with language are the basis of postmodern thought—the comfort of the unknown and the unpredictable and human/more-than-human relationships—and good teachers tap into this by default and often times automatically. What this means for research and praxis on engagement is that more focus needs to be placed on the relationships between youth's meaning-making practices and the materialities and immaterialities with which they engage.

Linked to current curricular systems, these engagements ought to be considered as dimensions of competencies and outcomes in curricular documents, in ways that decentralize the sole focus on reading and composition as to include ways of being/knowing/doing (Kuby & Rowsell, 2017; Kuby, Spector & Thiel, 2018) with reading and composition. One way to decentralize this focus is to offer larger options and metaphorical thinking in higher education and pre-service teacher training. For example, in the graduate and undergraduate courses I teach in Secondary English Language Arts Methods, I often refer to the idea of the curriculum as a metaphor for an art canvas. The implications of mentioning this metaphor to my students are two-fold: (1) it helps pre-service teachers build on their creativity to come up with original teaching strategies and methods, and (2) it allows them to remain hopeful and not feel restricted by the parameters of specific outcomes. Teachers' and pre-service teachers' hopes lie in their aspirations and curiosities about themselves and what drives them to teach—they reinvest such aspirations in the content that they teach as they engage with parts and layers of themselves (White & Lemieux, 2017).

Engagement↔Flow: From Metacognition to Posthuman Thought (1990–Present)

There are several theories that frame engagement as a metacognitive state in literacy studies. Although not specifically targeted to reading, Csikszentmihalyi's (1990) flow theory pertains to one's state of engagement during an activity pursued for its own sake. To me, an engaged reader is immersed in the activity as one loses track of time, lives something outside of the everyday reality, knows that one has the skills to do the task, and undergoes what Csikszentmihalyi (1990) calls an optimal experience.

In a recent chapter on the conditions for reading and attaining flow, Csikszentmihalyi (2014) argued that children and youth need to be taught reading in a way that develops the state of being *immersed* in reading. He further defended that situated reading engagement tendencies depend on the ability to be both challenged by the narrative and confident enough to develop comprehension and meaning-making. In another article on engagement, D. Shernoff, Csikszentmihalyi, Schneider, and E. Shernoff (2003) specify: "issuing appropriate challenges and providing opportunities to enhance skills [...] may be one of the most ideal ways of engaging students" (p. 160). Considering engagement and genre, more recent empirical research has shown how agency and choice played a large role in reading engagement, especially as it pertains to "disturbing books" (Ivey & Johnston, 2018) and trauma literature (Dutro, 2017; Radstone, 2007; Zembylas, 2015).

However, the main challenge in flow is to foster a good balance between the difficulties that the reading task requires and the skills that the reader possesses (see, for example, the dichotomy between skills and challenges). For Csikszentmihalyi, intrinsically motivated actions take place because of readers' interest in the reading act. The incentive is the experience of involvement itself as it provides immersion in the narrative, identification with characters, an immaterial relationship with text. This is when flow reaches its optimal state, where one is completely immersed in the activity one is completing.

As I have just broached the notion of motivation, I will now address important historical distinctions that emerged in the 1990s between reading engagement, reading motivation, and interest in reading, so as to clarify commonly used terms in reading engagement studies. Reading engagement envelops more than one term, such as motivated reading, strategic reading, pleasure in reading, reading achievement, and so forth (cf. Reinking, 2001; Guthrie & Wigfield, 2000). For example, Parsons (2006) puts several words together in the following excerpt. However, the first sentence focuses on reading interest, while the following one is oriented towards reading engagement:

> The more readers are able to elaborate on the images they have created, the more concrete the story world becomes for them and **the greater their comprehension and interest** (Guthrie & Anderson, 1999; Many & Wiseman, 1992). Hibbing and Rankin-Erickson (2003) observed that **engaged readers** spontaneously visualize what they read, recognizing a breakdown in images as an indication that they need to monitor their comprehension. (p. 493)

Here, the common denominator is readers' capacity to visualize fictional images, a category of reading engagement that has also been identified more recently by other reading research scholars (Kucirkova, Littleton & Cremin, 2016; Langlade, 2013; Massie, Boran & Wilhelm, 2014). One assumes that the author intends the same meaning in both sentences, despite the terms reading interest and reading engagement being used interchangeably. Thus, this example serves as a reason why it is important to clearly establish these distinctions.

Looking across reading engagement studies, two schools of thought govern the topic of reading engagement. One endorses the standardized measurement of reading engagement, as evidenced by studies on the development of Concept-Oriented Reading Instruction (CORI) to increase reading comprehension, motivation, and engagement in reading among adolescents (Guthrie & Cox, 2001; Guthrie & Wigfield, 1997; Wigfield et al., 2008). These dimensions are embedded within behavioral engagement stream. The other looks at students' reading experiences in relation to reading engagement, which is related to the state of flow and optimal experiences, and more emotional and embodied states of engagement (Csikszentmihalyi, 1990, 1997, 2003, 2014). To consider posthumanism as part of this discourse would be implementing the work of deconstructionists such as Gilles Deleuze, Félix Guattari, the later work of Roland Barthes, and that of Paul Ricoeur. I provided an overview of the posthumanism perspective early on, but for the time being, it is my understanding that behavioral studies on reading engagement have been beneficial to curriculum studies in ways that allowed for standardized testing and scoring across grades.

To further elaborate on the types of reading engagement in research, in their article on the role of reading engagement in reading comprehension, Wigfield et al. (2008) established three distinct types of reading engagement:

1. behavioral engagement, where students perform school tasks;
2. cognitive engagement, where students use complex strategies to "foster deep learning" (p. 432); and
3. emotional engagement, where students seemingly enjoy school tasks and show their enthusiasm for learning.

In a book chapter called "Promoting Reading Motivation," Guthrie and Knowles (2001) suggested a similar view of reading engagement: "engaged reading refers to the fusion of cognitive strategies, conceptual knowledge, and motivational goals during reading" (p. 159). Thus, reading engagement, as it is generally defined in the empirical realm, reveals that readers use all sorts of cognitive reading strategies to gain knowledge as well as motivational processes to be engaged. The social aspect has been included in other studies in the mid-1990s and the beginning of the 2000s (e.g., Guthrie, 1996; Guthrie & Wigfield, 2000). To corroborate the validity of the definition, I identified an extensive number of representative reading engagement definitions below (Table 2.1). Again, the common ground between these definitions is the focus on motivation (or motivational processes) and cognitive strategies for meaning-making. In two instances, the role of the social context for reading engagement was mentioned (see Guthrie, 1996; Guthrie & Wigfield, 2000). Gaining conceptual knowledge is also highlighted as a part of that type of engagement with narratives.

Drawing on these definitions of reading engagement, there is evidence (Guthrie & Knowles, 2001; Guthrie & Wigfield, 1997) that reading motivation has a noticeable influence on reading engagement. As Guthrie and Knowles (2001) noted: "motivation can be regarded as the individual's reason for engaging in reading" (p. 160). The type of motivation that is described here operates on a binary scheme (intrinsic vs. extrinsic), and there exist nine different ways to

Table 2.1: Reading engagement definitions primarily conducted by Guthrie and Wigfield.

Author(s) (year)	Definitions of reading engagement
Guthrie (1996)	"it depicts the learner as possessing a variety of **motivations to gain conceptual understanding** by using **cognitive competencies** and participating in a diversity of **social** interchanges" (p. 434)
Guthrie, Alverson & Poundstone (1999)	"engaging students in reading, then, involves attending to **motivation**, supportive **cognitive strategies** for reading, and enabling students to build a knowledge base for launching future reading events" (p. 8)
Guthrie & Cox (2001)	"By 'engaged readers,' we refer to students who are intrinsically **motivated** to read for the knowledge and enjoyment it provides. But engaged readers are also strategic. They use **strategies** such as self-monitoring and inferencing to understand text." (p. 284)
Guthrie et al. (1998)	"engagement in reading refers to the **motivated use of strategies** to gain **conceptual knowledge** during reading" (p. 261)
Guthrie & Wigfield (2000)	"engaged readers in the classroom or elsewhere coordinate their **strategies and knowledge** (**cognition**) within a community of literacy (**social**) in order to fulfill their personal goals, desires, and intentions (**motivation**)" (p. 404)
Wigfield & Guthrie (1997)	"In the engagement perspective on reading, both **cognitive** and **motivational** aspects of reading are considered" (p. 14)
Wigfield et al. (2008)	"when readers are fully engaged in reading they **comprehend** better, use **reading strategies** effectively, and are **motivated** to read" (p. 433)

nurture them. Guthrie and Knowles (2001) distinguish extrinsic from intrinsic motivation for engaged reading. The former refers to "external awards as goals for reading" (p. 160), such as encouragement, an incentive, or prize from a parent, or teacher. The latter is a motivation that comes from within, for example, the will to master a task as to become 'fluent' or 'expert': "it is the desire to be engaged in a task for its own sake rather than for a reward" (p. 160). The other three dimensions are the ones I previously outlined in the definitions from the work of Guthrie and Wigfield. The cognitive strategies refer to the processes of self-monitoring, comprehension, and meaning-making. The social aspect requires conversations and discussions with others. Finally, conceptual knowledge shows that reading is "knowledge-driven" (Guthrie & Wigfield, 2000, p. 417). While these dimensions are established and explained from behavioral and cognitivist stances, they are necessary and quite useful to understand how reading might happen when is it seen from that categorized standpoint.

Gambrell and Marinak (1997) have shown that there are appropriate external incentives that spark intrinsic motivation in reading, such as tangible ones offered as a reward for having achieved a determined set of goals. Praise and positive feedback are incentives (defined as intangible rewards) that may also impact one's intrinsic motivation to read. Similarly to the findings of Guthrie and Wigfield (2000), extrinsic and intrinsic motivation led to engagement in this study, as they identified how incentives can lead to deeper engagement in reading.

In a more extensive study, Guthrie and Wigfield (2000) refer to reading motivation as one's "personal goals, values, and beliefs with regard to the topics, processes, and outcomes of reading" (p. 405). The values can range from excitement to determination and hard work. While my view of reading engagement is different—as in, I see it as part of posthuman thought and holistic education—I recognize how their definition of reading motivation has been quite useful for reading engagement studies, as it encompasses intrinsic, extrinsic, and social motivation, motivational goals, and self-efficacy—dimensions that have been researched more extensively over the last 25 years.

My years of research on reading engagement have made it so that I situated myself in the qualitative realm, more specifically adopting phenomenological and ethnographic stances when looking at reading experiences (Lemieux & White, 2017). If we look at my understanding of reading engagement from a quantitative stance, it coincides with what Guthrie and Wigfield (and many other scholars) call *involvement in reading*. Involvement in reading is described as fulfilling intrinsic motivational goals, and it is very similar to Csikszentmihalyi's concept of optimal experience. Guthrie and Wigfield (1997) give examples of what involvement in reading looks like within their Motivations for Reading Questionnaire (MRQ) strategy: "I enjoy a long, involved story or fiction book/I feel like I make friends with people in good books/I like mysteries" (p. 24). There are different ways to look at how students channel and catalyze those experiences, and over the years I have situated myself within a phenomenological framework to detail how reading is experienced through mapping.

Other scholars have worked on clarifying these definitions. For example, Schallert and Reed (1997) offer a distinction among motivation, interest, engagement, and involvement in reading. For them, engagement embodies "a set of activity-related processes rather than a psychological state" (p. 69), the psychological state here perhaps referring to Csikszentmihalyi's state of flow and related concepts that delve into metacognition. Schallert and Reed (1997) build on Guthrie and Wigfield's (1997) work and describe engagement as the activity that combines reading strategies and motivation. Thus, they acknowledge that motivation is part of engagement, and distance these notions from interest, which is "less volitional" and "a trigger to attention deployment with the effect of aiding memory for material" (p. 70). Their understanding of involvement in reading is also very similar to that of Guthrie and Wigfield's (1997), but Schallert and Reed (1997) establish an important distinction between engagement and involvement:

> We see involvement as a special type of engagement. Engagement subsumes involvement in the sense that it is possible to be engaged without experiencing much involvement in a task, but it is not possible to be involved in a task without first being engaged. (p. 70)

In this quantitative, behavioral tradition of framing reading research, these authors see involvement as a sub-category of engagement, and link it to the experience of reading through dedication to the task and active meaning-making: "when we say a student is involved in a story, we mean that he or she is focusing on the reading to the exclusion of other tasks" (p. 70). I have doubts that involvement is subjugated to this autonomous, almost robotic understanding of involvement in reading. I remain unsure to this day that reading can exclude other tasks, given the multimodal and rhizomatic world in which we live, where reading is mostly social and driven by other tasks. At the time when this definition was crafted, in the mid-1990s, the internet was in dial-up mode and those connections could not be made. Now, adolescent readers read mostly on phones, except in the context of classroom assignments. Even in these cases, the reading task is never fully disconnected from other tasks.

In a similar manner, this understanding of involvement coincides with that of Csikszentmihalyi's (2014) state of the flow of reading, as one becomes focused on the reading act and loses track of time. The objective of pointing out this distinction is to highlight that there is not a clear consensus on the nature of reading engagement among researchers working in the field of reading research.

Having recently worked on and expanded my knowledge of posthumanism, and conducting research within a phenomenological tradition, it is my understanding that reading engagement goes beyond a single, identified focus on the task of reading. I frame reading engagement as the open result of an aesthetic, pluri-dimensional engagement—a holistic immersion—in reading. It is unpredictable and comes in waves, which are also unpredictable. It is a way to be in silent (sometimes vocal) conversation with the other (the author), others (thoughts that bring up others), and the self (see Bakthin's dialogism, for example). When one is engaged in reading, thoughts emerge and they can be identified or not. Bodily movements and expressions can be part of that process. It presupposes a sense of *being-with* that posthumanism assumes (Braidotti, 2013; Kuby & Rowsell, 2017; Nayar, 2014); being-with thoughts, the un/comfortable, the yet-to-be, the tangible, the pre-reflective, the affective, and the cognitive. It does not exclude, nor does it pretend to be exclusionary. More importantly, it focuses on parts of the self that are expressive[6] and expressed *at times* in reading response; and parts of the self that are based on more private moments of reading and perceptions of events. Those perceptions are framed by our backgrounds, culture/s, apprehensions of language/s, status, and other ontological dimensions (Rosenblatt, 1978). It echoes the early work of Bodgan (1992) on aesthetic and literary engagement, which is close to the notion of reading involvement described above: "the engaged reader, untidy and unpredictable, is amenable to, indeed embraces, the admixture of personal experience with the literary object unleashed by the recursive processing of text" (p. 109). As such, my understanding of reading engagement works closely with aesthetic engagement in reading.

Inevitably, Guthrie and Wigfield's work shows a solid tradition of causalities between reading engagement and such factors as reading motivation and achievement. There are many merits to this approach, such as the very useful pre- and post-questionnaires they developed for understanding students' reading motivations (Wigfield & Guthrie, 1997), or the Reading Engagement Index (REI) they used to quantitatively measure students' reading engagement in classroom contexts, according to the perspective of the teacher (Wigfield et al., 2008). In the same study where the REI was attributed, students were given a series of comprehension tests (such as the Gates-MacGinitie reading test) and performance assessments. The study pointed to valuable activities to assess engagement from a quantitative stance.

As Graesser and D'Mello (2012) point out, "the challenge lies in predicting when flow states occur. Perhaps this occurs when the text is at the reader's zone of optimal challenge: not too easy or too difficult, *but just right*" (p. 239, my emphasis). We all strive to know what the 'just right' is for our students, and standardized testing has generated multiple attempts to find that state. But to me, the concrete manifestation of this state might occur when readers become aware of their experiences and make sense of them through articulating or, in my case, mapping them on paper.

As I have explained in this section, the term 'engagement' remains complex; it resists a universal definition. Recent findings from Parsons and Taylor (2011) indicate that student input needs to be present to arrive at viable definitions of

6. I rely on Zahavi's definition of expressions to frame what I mean by states of engaged reading. According to Zahavi: "expressions refer to a verbal and non-verbal behaviour, such as facial expressions, gestures, bodily posture, or vocalization, by means of which mental states are revealed and displayed or communicated to others" (p. 184). This definition speaks to the many dispositions through which one may experience reading.

engagement: "More recently, researchers are asking students and teachers how *they* would measure engagement: this refocused question is producing both interesting qualitative criteria and differing definitions of engagement in learning, which, consequently, has had some impact on how we 'assess' learning" (pp. 3–4, author's emphasis). I have thus embraced this perspective in my research and asked students what *they* thought reading engagement was. In our 2017 study (White & Lemieux, 2017), one of the male participants, Tim explained that for him, reading engagement meant "reading on a regular basis," while Peter stated that it was "picturing the story in his mind." Undoubtedly, it is my view that Tim's definition is just as valid as Peter's, even though they understand reading engagement differently. Students should be the ones showing us what reading engagement means, as they are the ones doing the reading and sharing how they are feeling and perceiving engagement. Without readers' input, the very reading engagement we aim to measure becomes void, depleted of meaning. Reading engagement is thus the process of being involved in reading through an understanding of students' experiences with reading and the instances where students self-evaluate their engagement in reading.

This is where posthumanism becomes an important feature of engagement; as aesthetic experiences materialize in readers' minds, they are with their thoughts and they can expand on them or let them be. The nature of these thoughts matters less than the awareness of them in the engagement process.

Aesthetic Experiences and Reading Engagement

A number of researchers and philosophers (cf. Carroll, 2001; Dewey, 1943; Shusterman, 2008) over the years have turned their attention to the study of aesthetic experience. In his chapter "On the Scope of Aesthetic Experience," Seel (2008) defines an aesthetic experience as an "aesthetic perception" (p. 99) with the attributes of an event, where the event is historical-cultural and becomes meaningful through time for the individual. This definition puts a strong emphasis on a reader's perceptivity and subjectivity, and posits that aesthetic experiences are *shaped* by the individual's background (Rosenblatt, 1978). Other scholars (Abram, 1996; Shusterman, 2008) echo this statement and conceptualize the aesthetic experience as a phenomenological experience that is distinctly felt, though it may vary in intensity. The awareness that comes with phenomenology is linked to posthumanism; as one experiences and reflects on his reading, he is cohabiting with his thoughts. He shapes his thoughts and reversely he is shaped by his thoughts. I understand these experiences as *emerging from* the individual's transactions with the text.

More precisely, other avenues in reading research, as seen in studies conducted by Ahr and Joole (2013), suggest that aesthetic experiences can be felt on three levels of awareness:

1. Within the realm of "fictional activity" (Langlade, 2013), where the reader creates his own text[7] (also called reader's text/*texte de lecteur*).
2. Within a new perspective on the world (also called literary imagination; see also Stornaiuolo & Whitney's 2018 article on the practice of writing as worldmaking).
3. Through intersubjective discussions.

White (2007) identifies another type of awareness, one that results from individual experiences, as defined by combined moments of response prompted in aesthetic-oriented activities, and that focuses on values: "aesthetic education is about education in values awareness" (p. 5).

These levels of awareness, although well delimited, are not mutually exclusive. That is, they might happen simultaneously (e.g., Ahr & Joole's (2013) in the first and second dimensions, or complementarily (e.g., White's (2007) and Ahr and Joole's (2013) third dimension). In learning activities that foster these types of aesthetic experiences, awareness plays an important role in reading engagement (Ahr & Joole, 2013, p. 144). More attention ought to be given to these relationships, with a focus on fostering aesthetic experiences and different traces of reading engagement.

Building on these definitions, which derive from the fields of philosophy and language arts, I envision a strong connection between aesthetic experiences and reading engagement in language arts classes. To encourage this approach, I find teachers can foster aesthetic experiences of literature (in its multimodal or monomodal forms) and lead students to articulate their responses to artworks. The aesthetic dimension of the reaction becomes vital for holistic grasping, *living-through* and *living-with* literature. Without the aesthetic stance, one can *know about* books without *living-through* them. That is, no aesthetic engagement can take place: "One can demonstrate familiarity with a wide range of literary works, be a judge of craftsmanship, and still remain, from the point of view of a rounded understanding of art, aesthetically immature" (Rosenblatt, 1976, p. 52).

Through an aesthetic lens, reading engagement requires awareness of, and attention to, the delicate, fleeting intricacies of the reading transaction. Within that transaction, aesthetic experiences might take place and set the grounds for

7. Fictional activity consists of (1) fantastical activity (*activité fantasmatique*), where the reader uses his imaginary world to create meaning from the text; (2) mimetic coherence (*cohérence mimétique*), where the reader establishes causalities between character's actions or events in the narrative; (3) axiological judgement (*jugement axiologique*), where the reader morally judges character's actions or motives; and (4) visual realization (*concrétisation imageante*), where the reader sees the text through personal images and sounds.

moments of response that can serve as indicators for a holistic engagement (as in an embodiment or absorption) in reading. Aesthetic engagement in reading is an important step in a reader's meaning-making of the text because it raises awareness of one's feelings, and can lead to peer discussions that have the potential to shed light on different perspectives on the text. Nussbaum (1998) argues in favor of this type of engagement, as it allows readers to develop their narrative imagination, which in turn helps them make connections and note the differences between themselves and the text. It must be said that, since aesthetic experiences are subjective and individual, they are unpredictable, which means they are difficult to assess for teachers and researchers who are used to rigid, one-answer-possible methods. However, as McGee (1992) explains,

> Our biggest challenge then, is not to search 'to find the *right* way to teach a book, the *right* questions to ask, the *right* messages to underline, the *right* analysis to make' (Gardner, 1988), but rather to consider purposes for instruction and continue to seek new understandings that will inform our thinking about children, literature, and reading. (p. 529, author's emphasis)

In light of pedagogical tendencies driven by standardized testing, new understandings—such as allowing space for aesthetic experiences—lay the grounds for rich learning opportunities. As Bresler and Macintyre Latta (2008) point out: "the challenge that students encounter when making, perceiving, and sharing their aesthetic representations enrich their understandings of reading comprehension in ways that traditional types of assignments and assessments would not compare" (p. 20). When students are encouraged to focus on sharing their aesthetic experiences, they are more likely to deepen their reading perspectives, thus providing more pathways to engagement. The role of teachers becomes more focused on students' experiences, allowing for dialogue and interpretation. As White (2013) explains, "the role of the educator is not to pass definitive judgment upon the worth of a particular artwork; rather, it is to provide opportunities for sharing individuals' interpretations" (p. 113). Therefore, the investigation of aesthetic experiences and the ways they are shared in classroom contexts become important for engagement.

In language arts, and multimodality altogether, the aesthetic has proven to be one of the most important denominators for engagement (Burn & Kress, 2018). In a study on ways of providing students with aesthetically engaging learning experiences, Uhrmacher (2009) corroborates the finding that aesthetic learning experiences give way to meaning-making and engagement. Acknowledging that aesthetic experiences have their roots in the arts, Moroye and Uhrmacher (2012) state that these experiences "extend to all avenues of life, including learning. At such times when so engaged, we often lose ourselves in our task at-hand forgetting about time and daily concerns" (p. 65). Moroye and Uhrmacher's (2012) aesthetic learning experiences reflect Csikszentmihalyi's (1990) optimal experiences (where time goes by without a person noticing). The authors further elaborate six main dimensions of the conditions of aesthetic experiences for engagement: (1) connections, (2) risk-taking, (3) imagination, (4) sensory experiences, (5) perceptivity, and (6) active engagement.

The 'connections' dimension refers to the intellectual, social, emotional, communicative, or sensorial (Csikszentmihalyi & Robinson, 1990) ways the learner engages with the material, while 'risk-taking' represents creative strategies that drive students out of their common realm of experience. Moroye and Urmacher (2012) perceive read-alouds as risk-taking activities. If the purpose of risk-taking is to guide students in new ways of meaning-making, then I envision aesthetigram-making as one such activity. As such, in an article by White and Tompkins (2005) on a student's interaction with a large, modern bronze sculpture, the authors demonstrated that aesthetigram-mapping, at first unknown territory, ended up being a comfortable strategy to make meaning of the artwork. If aesthetigram-making involves risk, and has shown to be a successful method in visual art (White, 1998, 2007, 2011; White & Lemieux, 2017; White & Tompkins, 2005), then I argue that risk can also be taken in language arts, for students might undergo some level of aesthetic experiences when reading (see also the work on trauma literatures and affect by such literacy scholars as Dernikos, 2018; Dutro, 2017; Leander & Boldt, 2013).

The third dimension, 'imagination,' refers to the reader's ability to manipulate ideas creatively. In classroom settings, imagination can be prompted by questions that lead to its development (e.g., "describe your symbiotic *I-Thou* relationship with the text" (cf. White, 2013) or intuitive, self-prompted as a follow-up activity to the reception of an artwork, for instance). The fourth dimension, 'sensory experience,' takes place when one draws on one's multi-sensory attributes to interact with the object. Fifth, 'perceptivity' refers to a "deepened sensory experience" (p. 66), for example, resulting from a sustained and elongated observation of an aspect of the text.

Finally, active engagement empowers students as they are fully immersed in experiences when participating in a learning task: "Whether engrossed in a text or writing an expository essay, students who are actively engaged do not struggle to find relevance because their experience is meaningful in and of itself" (Moroye & Urmacher, 2012, p. 66). I found that some scholars define the parameters of aesthetic experiences in very permeable and open ways. As an example, Shusterman (2008) defines aesthetic experience as a cause of perception, and this happens through imagination. In another instance, White (2013) conceives imagination as intrinsically linked to the ability to make connections: "Aesthetically-oriented cognition involves imagination. By 'imagination' I mean a capacity to make connections" (p. 101). A third standpoint would be Maxine Greene's (1991) explanation that both categories of perception and imagination in the aesthetic experience "enlarge the scope of freedom for the individual" (p. 158).

In other words, Moroye and Urmacher's (2012) categories are not static, they are rather open and inclusive. One can undergo aesthetic experiences with several of these concepts and be engaged in reading that way. As such, research on aesthetigram-making (White, 1998, 2007, 2011; White & Lemieux, 2017; White & Tompkins, 2005) has provided useful insights into capturing moment-by-moment responses to artworks, and through the study of these maps, the multifaceted nature of aesthetic experiences emerge. Nonetheless, these potential conditions for engagement must be considered and implemented, especially in classroom settings, because they set the stage for valuing and encouraging aesthetic experiences.

Abbs's (1991) chapter "Defining the Aesthetic Field" establishes a coherent relationship between reading engagement and aesthetic experiences. Abbs (1991) first distinguishes aesthetics from aesthetic response. The former "denotes a mode of sensuous knowing essential for the life and development of consciousness" (p. 245), while the latter "is inevitably, through its sensory and physical operations, cognitive in nature" (p. 246). In other words, the aesthetic dimension encompasses necessary attributes of the aesthetic experience: to be aware and conscious of our meaning-making of the world, we must undergo these experiences at some point and be provided with opportunities to reflect upon them. Those conditions are present in posthumanist thought, for awareness becomes the first step towards engagement, and being-with is also part of that equation. As a reader engages in the habit of creating some distance by reflecting on what he reads, he evolves with his thoughts and has the ability to modify them or rest with them in the process.

Further on in the chapter, Abbs (1991) introduces the notion of aesthetic field, which he defines as:

> An intricate web of energy where the parts are seen in relationship, in a state of reciprocal flow between tradition and innovation, between form and impulse, between the society and the individual, between the four phases of *making, presenting, responding,* and *evaluating*, which mark the four essential elements of the aesthetic field. (p. 248, author's emphasis)

Abbs' aesthetic field depicts a series of invisible relationships between dimensions in which meaning-making occurs. *Making* refers to the act of creating the artwork (e.g., a writer's narrative composition). It is thus focused on the writer's work rather than that of the reader. *Presenting* underlines the necessary presence of an audience within the aesthetic encounter. As Abbs (1991) puts it: "No audience—no aesthetic" (p. 251), a statement that echoes Aristotle's early concerns for the audience's presence and its response. Considering this, the reader plays an important role insofar as he completes the artwork. This view reminds us of Rosenblatt's (1978) transactional theory, where a narrative only makes sense when it is read. Like Rosenblatt, Abbs (1991) conceives response as a crucial part of the aesthetic field and explains that *responding* covers the ways in which one reacts to an artwork. I am inclined to think that these reactions range from impulsively formulated responses to intuitive or partial ones, but Abbs (1991) defines them specifically as "intuitive apprehensions working through our senses and our feelings" (p. 252). *Evaluating* is meant to express one's transaction with the artwork, that is, to elaborate aesthetic responses. The author estimates that this fourth action is based on judgment. This notion of evaluating calls to mind a detachment (or distance); that is, the reader is in a position of reflection on his aesthetic experiences. As a post-event act, this reflection (or detachment) fosters deeper engagement: "In the best evaluation, there is actually a further engagement: the intellectual and the aesthetic combine to *make sense* of the sensuous. Evaluation makes *intelligible* (and communicable) the aesthetic response" (Abbs, 1991, p. 254, author's emphasis). Thus, according to Abbs (1991), all these cumulative steps are related to engagement.

Aesthetic experiences are highly qualitative in nature. As Berleant (2000) indicates, "Much of what we can point out in describing aesthetic experience follows from its qualitative character […] sensuous, as immediate, unique, noncognitive, intrinsic, and situational" (p. 92). These qualitative aesthetic experiences are lived by readers and then expressed in the form of aesthetic responses. The articulation of responses requires a detachment from the experience itself, which is nevertheless a necessary aspect to foster engagement (Brothers, 2014). For engagement to occur, aesthetic experiences and the subsequent detachment articulated through aesthetic responses need to be complementary. That is, they do not occur at the same time. As Bodgan (1992) notes: "to be engaged in experience and to be fully conscious of the act of experiencing at the same time is a psychological impossibility" (p. 110). The argument here is that the mind is awakened by the reading act through, for instance, narrative imagination (Nussbaum, 1998), but there ought to be a detachment at some point in order to further the process of engagement. That distance happens when there is an awareness of the lived aesthetic experiences, not only by the articulation of responses, but also through the sharing with others by means of class discussions.

I acknowledge that the reading transaction presupposes that engaged readers undergo reading experiences that oscillate between efferent and aesthetic stances

(Rosenblatt, 1976). However, limitations ensue as some readers might experience disengaged feelings like boredom, frustration, or even confusion (Graesser & D'Mello, 2012). Boredom will likely be felt if the material is too dense (low skills, low challenges), while anxiety (low skills, high challenges), or even relaxation (high skills, low challenges) might be experienced depending on the reader's skills and perceived challenges when engaging in an activity (Shernoff, Csikszentmihalyi, Schneider & Shernoff, 2003). In my research, I investigate the relationship between aesthetic experiences and engagement by guiding students in their awareness of their reactions towards the object to which they are reacting, whether these reactions are positive or negative. Even if some students show either apathy or relaxation in their early reactions (as tracked in their list of reactions and subsequent aesthetigrams), it marks a starting point for this awareness. When students list their reactions and chart them in maps, they become engaged in the process (White, 1998, 2007, 2011; White & Lemieux, 2017). I argue that this meaning-making might show traces of engagement, and that this engagement is defined by students themselves, not only through their aesthetic experiences but also through the articulation of what they think engagement is.

Thus, aesthetic experiences play a considerable role in that conception of engagement, as they are phenomenologically-oriented and posthumanely-driven. As Langlade (2006) posits: "any literary reading activity presupposes the more or less conscious development of strategies; consequently all analyses of reading experiences aim to show reading strategies, that is, the ways in which the reader makes sense of the text" (p. 56, my translation). In light of this focus on meaning-making, I understand aesthetigram-making as both a teaching and a research strategy on which to base patterns of engagement. I also acknowledge that, for some students, it will not be easy to experience an aesthetic transaction with the text, but at the same time there exist conditions that might facilitate that engagement. These include developing an openness to the experience or selectively focusing on the first pages of a novel or the first minutes of a film (Fenner, 2010), and attending to one's narrative imagination (Nussbaum, 1998). Even if that openness cannot be guaranteed, my aim is to show pathways that offer that possibility. In the next paragraphs, I present another aesthetic-oriented strategy that might facilitate reading engagement.

For a long time, I have been interested in providing educators with concrete ways to understand students' aesthetic, emotional, and intellectual responses to literature and film. It is important to emphasize such components of reading engagement because reading implies key student skills development, such as the development of: social imagination (Lysaker & Miller, 2012); empathy (Lemieux, 2015; Muth, 2016); improved literacy skills (Sullivan & Brown, 2015); and even reading comprehension in other empirical studies (Cox & Guthrie, 2001). Further evidence points to the benefits of developing reading engagement in students because they develop strong predictors for reading attainment (Cremin, 2007, 2014), which are key objectives and foci of the Canadian schooling system. While my research does not focus on these relationships specifically, it offers qualitative insights into what reading engagement looks like in terms of varying degrees, and the nature of such moments of engagement. Rather, the framework that I present provides avenues that make us think about the ways we teach literature and gives clues as to how to foster literary experiences that increase self-awareness as one reads. As such, one of my previous studies looked at the development of male students' voices in literature classes, where they were encouraged to improve their reading engagement through reinforcing their response capacities. One of the broader implications of this study was that boys' reading engagement patterns show, in fact, that they are affective and emotional readers in high school settings, which may come as a surprise to some. I will exemplify this in upcoming chapters.

As explained earlier, there are many ways to understand and look at the question of reading engagement in high school settings. Looking across phenomenological theories (Husserl, 1982; Merleau-Ponty, 1962; Ricoeur, 1981, 1990; Van Manen, 1990, 2002, 2014) by specifically focusing on students' meaning-making through their response articulations, map-making, and creative writing skills. I previously used phenomenology as a lens to view students' responses. In other words, I did not discuss nor explain phenomenological concepts with the high school students who participated in this study. I was interested in the nature of students' responses because, in a classroom context where these are valued and discussed, students had the opportunity to expand upon them, thus potentially engaging further.

Teaching literature requires guiding students in their awareness of their perceptions and reactions as they read. To reify students' awareness of their own reactions, my research utilizes visual mapping as a pedagogical tool for fostering and preserving records of reactions to literary texts and films. In literature pedagogy and literacy studies, I find it useful to document such traces not only to cater to ministerial competencies and outcomes (e.g., the competency of helping students "react to text"), but also to encourage student voices during classroom discussions. These individual records enable teachers to be aware of their students' thought process and emotions when as they engage in a reading activity. Then, teachers can build on this knowledge to plan richer (and perhaps individually tailored) reading material and experiences for their students.

My review of reader-response and reading engagement theories from the last 20 years has addressed how the focus of students' aesthetic transactions precedes that of the aesthetic response—how these personal meaning-making instances, when tracked and brought to attention, have the potential to inform students' reading engagement. I also introduced two schools of thought regarding the meaning-making categories of encounters. The first one derives from visual arts and encourages participant-generated development of reading responses. The second stems from reading research and dictates the analysis through researcher-designed categories of readers' experiences. I have positioned myself in the former school, all the while recognizing the contributions of the latter.

Reader-viewer theory (Lebrun, Lacelle & Boutin, 2012) maintains that students construct meaning when they read, and they deconstruct and reconstruct that same meaning when they watch the eponymous film. I argue that films are efficient artworks to which students can respond, and through which they can undergo aesthetic experiences.

Several schools of thought (reading research behaviorists, psychologists, aestheticians, philosophers) define reading engagement differently. Behaviorists Guthrie and Wigfield conceive that cognitive strategies, social interactions, motivation, and concept knowledge play a large role in the construction of reading engagement, while psychologist Csikszentmihalyi sees reaching flow experiences (i.e., the balance between challenge and skills) as being the goal of engagement. The third conceptualization draws upon engagement (also called 'involvement' by behaviorists) as an immersion in reading, one that is phenomenologically-based and that brings forth the awareness of aesthetic experiences in textual transactions. The common ground between these three approaches to reading engagement is the need to get students active and implicated in the reading act. They differ in that the first focuses on processes, the second on skills, and the third on aesthetic awareness.

Reading engagement can be understood through the awareness of, and attention to, aesthetic experiences, which are developed in different spaces of transaction (e.g., fictional activity, literary imagination) and discussion (social aspects of sharing the experiences). Aesthetic experiences are related to engagement on several levels: through the reader's perception and ability to make connections and take risks, as well as through his imagination and sensory experiences. I acknowledge Bodgan's (1992) argument that engagement can be achieved through some kind of distance from the text, the exercise in aesthetigram-making notwithstanding.

Limits and Possibilities in Phenomenological Research

Phenomenology thus has several advantages and limitations. It offers an entry point into literacies that can be materialized through objects such as texts (Burnett, Merchant, Pahl & Rowsell, 2014) and affective states in third spaces, such as poetry (Sameshima, 2019). What I have highlighted so far is how phenomenology gives a privileged access into the experiences of student readers and its potential to inform teachers and researchers regarding how it *feels* to read (Leander et al., 2017). Then, in terms of challenges, I have mentioned elsewhere, with Boyd White, the problems phenomenology may cause for evaluation and the related validity of interpretations (Lemieux & White, 2017). Nevertheless, phenomenology shows promising avenues for insights into human consciousness, through descriptions of *life as lived* (Van Manen, 1990), which renders literacy meaningful. In phenomenology, human experiences determine the framework of the research and the point of collecting people's experiences is to "become more experienced ourselves" (Van Manen, 1990, p. 62). The task of the teacher is to know herself better, so that she can develop more in-depth knowledge of her students and their needs.

The Study: Navigating the Relational in Reader Engagement Post-2015

Observations on "Best Practices" to Develop Engaged Readers

There have been substantial debates regarding "best practices" to foster reading engagement (e.g., Guthrie and Wigfield's empirical orientation to the study of reading engagement as opposed to, for example, Bodgan and Nussbaum's approach on cultivating the imagination, or White's phenomenology regarding engagement). St. Clair (2005) warns that establishing "best practices" is risky, and even unreliable, for "there is no way to predict the emotional state of learners, and there will never be" (p. 447). Recent studies have maintained that such practices nonetheless exist (Gambrell & Mandel Morrow, 2014; Roskos & Neuman, 2014).

If we treat those practices as suggestions rather than doctrines (St. Clair, 2005), they become more flexible research guidelines. One suggestion is to ground reading engagement as a dynamic entity that can be visualized through mapping reactions to text. In a previous study (Lemieux, 2015), I proposed avenues to show traces of reading engagement in adolescent boys reading a play, *Incendies*, and responding to its written and adapted film versions. This study elaborated on a pedagogical sequence enabling students to show individual traces of reading engagement, rendered public through visual maps, and to articulate how those engagements manifest themselves on their maps.

I wish to specify that I do not pursue the relationship between reading competence, academic achievement, and instruction, as that relationship has been examined before (cf. Guthrie, 1996; Guthrie & Cox, 2001, Wigfield, 1997; Wigfield et al., 2008). Rather, in my study, I pursued phenomenological accounts of the activity of reading in a classroom context, focusing on boys' reactions to text and film. That is, my research emphasized the study of reading accounts as articulated by the participants themselves. In this sense, I adopt subjectively-oriented, as opposed to objectively-oriented conceptions of reading engagement. I provide additional examples of his later on in the book.

Boys often wear the unpopular label of "struggling readers." The implication of such a label is that they lack the awareness of possible connections between the text and their personal life (Cremin, 2014). So with this expanded study, I investigate the range and patterns of involvement in such connections (or lack thereof) in reading. Common research beliefs stem from the established repercussions of the *Matthew effect* (Stanovich, 1986), which stipulates that reading engagement develops at a young age, and those who were not read stories as children are unlikely to become fluent readers as they grow older. If this is so, then compounding the situation, secondary school teachers are required to show all students how to read, in times where reading instruction consists in "readicide" (Gallagher, 2009), that is "systematic[ally] killing […] the love of reading, often exacerbated by the inane, mind-numbing practices found in schools" (p. 2). Similar practices are adopted in Quebec, where reading tests are still handed out in schools, on occasion. In a case study examining literacy gender gaps in high school students, Sarroub and Pernicek (2016) contend that reading instruction for boys should not depend on standardized testing. Rather, teachers' attention should be directed towards students' lived lives and reading experiences, taking into consideration students' individual differences and subjectivities. My research takes the same position.

If Stanovich and Gallagher are correct, reading research needs to be concerned with other pedagogical strategies for developing reading involvement. But before we can develop those strategies, we need to understand the nature of interactions with literature that readers experience. The range of potential experiences can show the variety and complexity of moments that suggest engagement. This is the focus of my research.

Rationale for Using Film

I used film in this research project for various reasons. I describe them below. The use of multimodality in classroom settings, such as the use of film in addition to a written text, can enhance learning experiences (Erstad, 2013; Lemieux, Burkholder & Fonseca, 2019; Rowsell, 2013). When paired with student-oriented pedagogy (as opposed to more traditional, teacher-centred methods), film has proven to bolster student engagement on multiple occasions (Lemieux, 2015). For example, studies in the UK have been conducted on how high school students find films relatable, in the sense that they are viable sources to provide holistic understandings of narratives (Maine, 2015). Despite the occasional bad press whereby they provide simplified versions of printed stories, movies provide alternative worlds to which students can respond in similarly alternative ways, opening up discussions within themselves as readers and viewers, and among others as "experiencers" (my neologism) of narratives. In addition, many teachers and researchers have recommended film as a viable source for engagement in the literature classroom (Maine & Shields, 2015; Nixon & Comber, 2001).

Lacelle (2009) has done extensive work in literacy studies, and her research showed how high school female students responded to, and understood, print narratives in comparison to film narratives (the case of *Les portes tournantes*). This very useful study has developed a concrete model to capture evidence of reading-viewing in youth based on three theoretical streams: semiotics, cognition, and subjectivity. This study has influenced me in the way I understand text and read, and Lacelle's model (further synthesized in 2012) has particularly shaped how I position my research in the subjective stream. I deepened this stream with my study, looking at students' reception of a printed text and its eponymous film version. This exercise was not so much a comparison of versions, but more an exploration of the hubs of reception in both cases, observing what engagement looked like in each instance.

When students listen to and watch the film version, they have the potential to understand differently than when they are reading. For example, hearing some words might affect aesthetic reception and comprehension in literacy practices, especially in the context of classroom learning (cf. Low, Brushwood Rose & Salvio, 2017). What I take away from this study is the fact that film is an additional narrative for students to respond to, and they can do this in a different way. I frame it very similarly in the study that I describe later. That is, the additional visual and aural modes could resonate with students in different ways than written text. Mapping is one of the ways that they can arrive at those conclusions and share their experience.

In a recent study investigating three stances to interpret and look at multimodal data, Brushwood Rose and Low (2014) explain how visual methods may result in attention to affective qualities that otherwise remain evanescent or unseen. This procedure is made in an effort to render the invisible visible, all the while leaving the interpretation to the participant and the researcher (see also Kendrick & Rowsell, 2014 and Rowsell & Kendrick, 2013). In other words, visual methods, as well as visuals themselves, represent additional ways of portraying meaning-making—understandings that printed words sometimes cannot provide nor afford (Brushwood Rose & Low, 2014). In this sense, it is within the narrative of film and responses to the film narrative and printed narrative that I attempted to grasp the immateriality of literacy (Burnett, Merchant, Pahl & Rowsell, 2014). That is, I felt it was important to record those fleeting moments of response specifically because charting those responses involves participant agency. Such agency is crucial to literacy learning. Research often downplays the role of affect in literacy learning, and I argue that mapping can help develop expressions in reaction to narratives to which students are confronted in the high school literature classroom.

Contextualizing the Research

I conceptualize reading engagement similarly to those scholars who have undertaken studies on literary experiences of print-based and non-print-based artworks. For example, Iftody, Sumara, and Davis (2006) explain that reading engagement with fiction helps develop consciousness, which, in turn, heightens the relationship between the self and one's reading awareness. Since one of the purposes of aesthetigrams is to develop that consciousness and provide evidence of interaction patterns, my research creates insights into the phenomenological dialogue that Iftody, Sumara, and Davis (2006) describe. As such, "while some students are intuitively aware of these relationships, *most require careful guidance* in learning *how* to notice the deeper structures of literary forms and how these contribute to the ongoing creation of consciousness awareness" (p. 238, my emphasis). In other words, relating literature to life allows for identification with—and alternatively, alienation or distance from (at times when the reader does not see a reflection of himself in the narrative)—the characters within the narratives.

Teachers are striving to propel students' consciousness, and one effective way of doing so is through developing empathy. Relating literature to life lays the groundwork for embodied learning that may generate empathetic skills in readers (Bogdan, 1992; Bogdan, Cunningham & Davis, 2000; Brett, 2016; Larrivé, 2015; Lemieux, 2015; Nussbaum, 1998; Sumara, Luce-Kapler & Iftody, 2008). Identification with characters enables embodied learning insofar as one can experience through the characters' actions and words. And such identification implies that empathy has the potential to be developed in these conditions, if it is not already at work.

Scope and Boundaries

I must address in this section the aspects of reading engagement I am covering and those I am not. I explained earlier that I do not agree with the idea that degrees of reading engagement can solely be determined by standardized test criteria. I see reading engagement as the reader's involvement with the narrative, as demonstrated in follow-up activities (aesthetigram and/or subsequent creative ekphrastic writing). My epistemological rationale comes from phenomenological studies (Merleau-Ponty, 1962; Van Manen, 1990, 2014) and the overall underlying principle in Barthes' (1984) *Death of the Author,* which stipulates that the reader can only exist at the expense of the author's vanishing. In so doing, the reader can fully engage with fiction through his own lived experiences. Those lived experiences are the object of this research.

I borrow from Bogdan, Davis, and Robertson (1997) and conceptualize reading experiences as akin to viewing ones: "we treat 'viewing experience' as coterminous with 'reading' in the sense that both activities involve the active production of meaning through encounters with discourse" (p. 101, n. 1). In that sense, there is no separate protocol to keep track of viewing and reading experiences. The strategy is the same, but viewing adds an additional dimension that triggers different reactions. I nevertheless adapted the aesthetigram questionnaire in both reading and viewing activities in order to guide students in their meaning-making construction (e.g., I extrapolated the category of "stylistic preferences" to preferences regarding color, form, shape, in the viewing experience, and included figures of speech, sentence structure, and metaphors in the same category).

Furthermore, I am not addressing multimodal facets of viewing and meaning-making, such as the semiotics of the viewing activity. My focus is on students' lived experiences of text as taken in the broader sense. As such, I am not investigating aesthetigrams in their capacity to develop multimodal competencies, despite the useful contributions such research would entail. Further, my project did not tackle the sociocultural influence of peers. Finally, the study analyzed in Chapters Three and Four was conducted in a high school in the Greater Montreal Area. The findings cannot be generalized to all Montreal, Quebec, or Canadian high schools, because phenomenological replications at moments of reception are impossible. That said, the methods can be used in other settings that include, for example, readers' or viewers' receptions of texts.

Limitations

The study presented in Chapters Three and Four was conducted over six weeks. By definition, it is not a year-long reading research study, and results should not be expected to reflect the methods longitudinal studies require. The teacher with whom I worked was generous in giving me her time and in scheduling the research so it would make sense for her teaching, her students, and the research project. The results I present corresponds to eleven student aesthetigrams and one case study of the complete exercises that is representative of my sample. Nonetheless, the eleven aesthetigrams data point to students' categories of reactions in response to the scene of the play *Incendies* and the corresponding scene of the eponymous film.

Students did not focus on the book in its entirety. Such a task would have been well beyond the available timeframe of this study. In terms of limitations, thus, this means that I am not doing a longitudinal study, and I take this as an opportunity to suggest further avenues for research. Thus, I am encouraging others interested in this type of work to explore reading engagement over longer periods of time. And since my research is classroom-based, it would be very useful to know what reading engagement looks like in informal settings (e.g., at home). This type of research would give important insight into post-curricular engagement methods outside schooling and school settings.

References

Abbs, P. (1991). Defining the aesthetic field. In R. A. Smith & A. Simpson (Eds.), *Aesthetics and arts education* (pp. 245–255). Urbana/Chicago: University of Illinois Press.

Abram, D. (1997). *The spell of the sensuous: Perception and language in a more-than-human world.* New York, NY: Vintage Books.

Ahr, S. & Joole, P. (2013). Transmission et expérience esthétique dans les premier et second degrés. In N. Rannou (Ed.), *L'expérience du sujet lecteur: travaux en cours* (pp. 133–145). Grenoble, France: Presses de l'Université de Grenoble.

Attridge, D. (2010). *Reading and responsibility: Deconstruction's traces.* Edinburgh, England: Edinburgh University Press.

Barad, K. (2007). *Meeting the universe halfway: Quantum physics and the entanglement of matter and meaning*. Durham, NC: Duke University Press.

Baroutsis, A. & Woods, A. (2018). Materialities, multiliteracies, and makerspaces: Design-based experiments in teacher/researcher collaborations. In N. Kucirkova, J. Rowsell & G. Fallon (Eds.), *International Handbook of Learning with Technology in Early Childhood.* New York, NY: Routledge.

Barthes, R. (1970). *S/Z*. Paris, France: Seuil.

Barthes, R. (1982). *L'obvie et l'obtus*. Paris, France: Seuil.

Barthes, R. (1984). La mort de l'auteur. In R. Barthes (Ed.), *Essais critiques IV : Le bruissement de la langue* (pp. 63–69). Paris, France: Seuil.

Berleant, A. (2000). *The aesthetic field: A phenomenology of aesthetic experience.* Christchurch, New Zealand: Cybereditions.

Bers, M. U. (2018). *Coding as playground: Programming and computational thinking in the early childhood classroom.* New York, NY: Routledge.

Bodgan, D. (1992). *Re-education the imagination: Towards a poetics, politics, and pedagogy of literary engagement.* Portsmouth, NH: Heinemann.

Bogdan, D., Cunningham, E. J. & Davis, H. E. (2000). Reintergrating sensibility: Situated knowledges and embodied readers. *New Literary History, 31*, 477–507.

Bogdan, D., Davis, H. E. & Robertson, J. (1997). Sweet surrender and trespassing desires in reading: Jane Campion's *The Piano* and the struggle for responsible pedagogy. *Changing English, 4*(1), 81–103.

Braidotti, R. (2013). *The posthuman.* Malden, MA: Polity.

Bresler, L. & Macintyre Latta, M. (2008). Venturing into unknown territory: Using aesthetic representations to understand reading comprehension. *International Journal of Education and the Arts, 9*(1), 1–23.

Brett, A. T. (2016). Seeking a balance: Discussion strategies that foster reading with authorial empathy. *Journal of Adult & Adolescent Literacy, 60*(3), 295–304.

Brothers, M. (2014). *Distance in preaching: Room to speak, space to listen.* Grand Rapids, MI: William B. Eerdmans.

Brushwood Rose, C. & Low, B. (2014). Exploring the 'craftedness' of multimedia narratives: From creation to interpretation. *Visual Studies, 29*(1), 30–39.

Burn, A. & Kress, G. (2018). Multimodality, style and the aesthetic: The case of the digital werewolf. In E. Tønnessen & F. Forsgren (Eds.), *Multimodality and aesthetics.* London: Routledge.

Burnett, C. (2015). (Im)materialising literacies. In J. Rowsell & K. Pahl (Eds.), *The Routledge Handbook of Literacy Studies* (pp. 520–531), New York, NY: Routledge.

Burnett, C., Merchant, G., Pahl, K. & Rowsell, J. (2014). The (im)materiality of literacy: The significance of subjectivity to new literacies research. *Discourse: Studies in the Cultural Politics of Education, 35*(1): 90–103.

Carroll, N. (2001). *Beyond aesthetics: Philosophical essays.* Cambridge, MA: Cambridge University Press.

Cox, C. & Guthrie, J. T. (2001). Motivational and cognitive contributions to students' amount of reading. *Contemporary Educational Psychology, 26*(1), 116–131.

Cremin, T. (2007). Reading for pleasure: Diversity, delight and desire. In K. Goouch & A. Lambirth (Eds.), *Understanding phonics and the teaching of reading* (pp. 166–190). Berkshire, England: McGraw-Hill.

Cremin, T. (2014). Reading for pleasure and reading engagement: Reviewing the research. In Cremin, T., Mottram, M., Collins, F. M., Powell, S. & Safford, K. (Eds.), *Building communities of engaged readers: Reading for pleasure* (pp. 5–20). London, England: Routledge.

Csikszentmihalyi, M. (1990). *Flow: The psychology of optimal experience.* San Francisco, CA: Harper Collins.

Csikszentmihalyi, M. (1997). *Finding flow: The psychology of engagement with everyday life.* New York, NY: Basic Books.

Csikszentmihalyi, M. (2003). *Good business: Leadership, flow, and the making of meaning.* New York, NY: Viking.

Csikszentmihalyi, M. (2014). Flow: The joy of reading. In M. Csikszentmihalyi (Ed.), *Applications of flow in human development and education* (pp. 227–240). New York, NY: Springer.

Csikszentmihalyi, M. & Robinson, R. (1990). *The art of seeing: An interpretation of the aesthetic encounter*. Malibu, CA: J. Paul Getty Trust.

Deleuze, G. & Guattari, F. (1991). *Qu'est-ce que la philosophie?* Paris: Éditions de Minuit.

Deprêtre, E. & Duarte, G.A. (2019). *Transmédialité, bande dessinée & adaptation*. Clermond-Ferrand : Presses universitaires Blaise Pascal.

Dernikos, B. P. (2018). 'It's like you don't want to read it again': Exploring affects, trauma and 'willful' literacies. *Journal of Early Childhood Literacy*. doi: 10.1177/1468798418756187

Dernikos, B. P. & Thiel, J. J. (2019). Literacy learning as cruelly optimistic: Recovering possible lost futures through transmedial storytelling. *Literacy*, 1–9. https://doi.org/10.1111/lit.12207

Dewey, J. (1943/1958). *Art as experience*. New York, NY: Capricorn Books.

Duchamp, M. (1922). Lits et ratures. Note 224, from Paul Matisse (*Marcel Duchamp : Notes*, 1980).

Dutro, E. (2017). Let's start with heartbreak: The perilous potential of trauma in literacy. *Language Arts*, *94*(5), 326–337.

Eaton, M. M. & Moore, R. (2002). Aesthetic experience: Its revival and its relevance to aesthetic education. *Journal of Aesthetic Education*, *36*(2), 9–23.

Ehret, C., Hollett, T. & Jocius, R. (2016). The matter of new media making: An intra-action analysis of adolescents making a digital book trailer. *Journal of Literacy Research*, *48*(3), 346–377.

Erstad, O. (2013). *Digital learning lives: Trajectories, literacies, and schooling*. New York, NY: Peter Lang.

Fenner, D. E. W. (2010). Context building and education imaginative engagement. *Journal of Aesthetic Education*, *44*(3), 109–123.

Gambrell, L. B. & Mandel Morrow, L. (2014). *Best practices in literacy instruction* (5th ed.). New York, NY: Guilford Press.

Gambrell, L. B. & Marinak, B. A. (1997). Incentives and intrinsic motivation to read. *Reading engagement: Motivating readers through integrated instruction* (pp. 205–217). Newark, DE: International Reading Association.

Gardner, H. (1988). Toward more effective arts education. *Journal of Aesthetic Education*, *22*(1), 157–167.

Graesser, A. C. & D'Mello, S. (2012). Moment-to-moment emotions during reading. *The Reading Teacher*, *66*(3), 238–242.

Greene, M. (1991). Aesthetic literacy. In R. A. Smith & A. Simpson (Eds.), *Aesthetics and arts education* (pp. 149–161). Urbana/Chicago: University of Illinois Press.

Greene, M. (1995). *Releasing the imagination: Essays on education, the arts and social change*. San Francisco, CA: Jossey-Bass.

Guthrie, J. T. (1996). Educational contexts for engagement in literacy. *The Reading Teacher*, *49*(6), 432–445.

Guthrie, J. T. & Anderson, E. (1999). Engagement in reading: Processes of motivated, strategic, knowledgeable, social readers. In J. T. Guthrie & D.E. Alvermann (Eds.), *Engaged Reading: Processes, Practices, and Policy Implications* (pp. 17–45). New York, NY: Teachers College Press.

Guthrie, J. T., Alverson, S. & Poundstone, C. (1999). Engaging students in reading. *Knowledge Quest, 27*(4), 8–16.

Guthrie, J. T. & Cox, K. E. (2001). Classroom conditions for motivation and engagement in reading. *Educational Psychology Review, 13*(3), 283–302.

Guthrie, J. T. & Knowles, K. T. (2001). Promoting reading motivation. In L. Verhoeven & C. Snow (Eds.), *Literacy and motivation: Reading engagement in individuals and groups* (pp. 159–176). Mahwah, NJ: Lawrence Erlbaum Associates.

Guthrie, J. T. & Van Meter, P., Hancock, G. R., McCann, A., Anderson, E. & Alao, S. (1998). Does concept-oriented reading instruction increased strategy use and conceptual learning from text? *Journal of Educational Psychology, 90*(2), 261–278.

Guthrie, J. T. & Wigfield, A. (1997). *Reading engagement: Motivating readers through integrated instruction*. Newark, DE: International Reading Association.

Guthrie, J. T. & Wigfield, A. (2000). Engagement and motivation in reading. In M. L. Kamil, P. B. Mosenthal, P. D., Pearson & R. Barr (Eds.), *Handbook of reading research*(Vol. III, pp. 403–422). Mahwah, NJ: Lawrence Erlbaum Associates.

Hackett, A. & Somerville, M. (2017). Posthuman literacies: Young children moving in time, place, and more-than-human worlds. *Journal of Early Childhood Literacy, 17*(3), 374–381.

Hawreliak, J. & Lemieux, A. (2020). The semiotics of social justice: A multimodal approach to examining social justice issues in videogames. *Discourse: Studies in the Cultural Politics of Education*.

Hibbing, A. N. & Rankin-Erickson, J. L. (2003). A picture is worth a thousand words: Using visual images to improve comprehension for middle school struggling readers. *The Reading Teacher, 56*(8), 758–770.

Husserl, E. (1931/1982). *Ideas I: General introduction to pure phenomenology*. New York, NY: Macmillan.

Iftody, T., Sumara, D. J. & Davis, B. (2006). Consciousness and the literary engagement: Toward a bio-cultural theory of reading and learning. *Language and Literacy, 8*(1), 1–24.

Ivey, G. & Johnston, P. (2018). Engaging disturbing books. *Journal of Adolescent & Adult Literacy, 62*(2), 143–150.

Kendrick, M. & Rowsell, J. (2014). The visual turn: Transitioning into visual approaches to literacy education. In D. Jarvis & S. B. Elliott-John (Eds.), *Perspectives on transitions in schooling and instructional practice* (pp. 320–345). Toronto, ON: University of Toronto Press.

Kuby, C. R. & Rowsell, J. (2017). Early literacy and the posthuman: Pedagogies and methodologies. *Journal of Early Childhood Literacy, 17*(3), 285–296.

Kuby, C. R., Spector, K., Thiel, J. (2018). *Posthumanism and literacy education: Knowing/becoming/doing literacies*. New York, NY: Routledge.

Kucirkova, N., Littleton, K. & Cremin, T. (2016). Young children's reading for pleasure with digital books: Six key facets of engagement. *Cambridge Journal of Education*, *47*(1), 67–84.

Lacelle, N. (2009). *Modèle de lecture-spectature, à intention didactique, de l'œuvre littéraire et de son adaptation filmique*. Thèse inédite. Montréal: Université du Québec à Montréal, Département des sciences de l'éducation.

Lacelle, N. (2012). Des propositions d'enseignement de lecture littéraire et filmique pour fonder une didactique de la lecture multimodale. In M. Lebrun, N. Lacelle & J.-F. Boutin (Eds.), *La littératie médiatique multimodale: De nouvelles approches en lecture-écriture à l'école et hors de l'école* (pp. 171–188). Québec, QC: Presses de l'Université du Québec.

Langlade, G. (2006). L'activité fictionnalisante du lecteur. In M. Braud, B. Laville & B. Louichon (Eds.), *Les enseignements de la fiction*. Bordeaux, France: Presses de l'Université de Bordeaux.

Langlade, G. (2013). Chartreuse(s) de Parme: D'une lecture subjective à l'autre. In N. Rannou (Ed.), *L'expérience du sujet lecteur: travaux en cours* (pp. 41–53). Grenoble, France: Presses de l'Université de Grenoble.

Larrivé, V. (2015). Empathie fictionnelle et écriture en « je » fictif. *Repères*, *51*, 157–176.

Leander, K. M., Aziz, S., Botzakis, S., Ehret, C., Landry, D. & Rowsell, J. (2017). Readings and experiences of multimodality. *Literacy Research: Theory, Method, and Practice*, *66*(1), 95–116.

Leander, K. M. & Boldt, G. M. (2013). Rereading "A pedagogy of multiliteracies": Bodies, texts, and emergence. *Journal of Literacy Research*, *45*(1), 22–46.

Lebrun, M., Lacelle, N. & Boutin, J.-F. (Eds.). (2012). *La littératie médiatique multimodale: De nouvelles approches en lecture-écriture à l'école et hors de l'école*. Québec, QC: Presses de l'Université du Québec.

Lemieux, A. (2015). Think it through: Fostering aesthetic experiences to raise interest literature at the high school level. *Journal of the Canadian Association of Curriculum Studies*, *12*(2), 66–93.

Lemieux, A. (2019). *X-Men Apocalypse*: The spaces between transmedia storytelling and transmedia characters. In E. Deprêtre & G. A. Duarte (Eds.), *Transmédialité, bande dessinée et adaptation* (pp. 245–256). Clermont-Ferrand, France: Presses universitaires Blaise Pascal.

Lemieux, A., Burkholder, C. & Ribeiro Fonseca, J. M. (2019). Pedagogies of empathy-building: Canadian and Azorean perspectives of film-viewing in higher education. In G. Barton & S. Garvis (Eds.), *Compassion and Empathy in Educational Contexts* (pp. 271–288). London, UK: Palgrave Macmillan.

Lemieux, A. & Rowsell, J. (2019). Digital technologies and online learning in secondary education (Canada). *Bloomsbury Education and Childhood Studies*, DOI: 10.5040/9781474209441.0038

Low, B., Brushwood Rose, C. & Salvio, P. M. (2017). *Community-based media pedagogies: Relational practices of listening in the commons*. New York, NY: Routledge.

Lyotard, J.-F. (1984). *The postmodern condition: A report on knowledge*. Minneapolis: University of Minnesota Press.

Lysaker, J. T. & Miller, A. (2012). Engaging social imagination: The developmental work of wordless book reading. *Journal of Early Childhood Literacy*, *13*(2), 147–742.

Maine, F. (2015). *Teaching comprehension through reading and responding to film*. Leicester, England: The United Kingdom Literacy Association.

Maine, F. & Shields, R. (2015). Developing reading comprehension with moving image narratives. *Cambridge Journal of Education, 45*(4), 519–535.

Many, J. E. & Wiseman, D. L. (1992). The effect of teaching approach on third-grade students' response to literature. *Journal of Reading Behavior, 24*(3), 265–287.

Massie, M., Boran, K. & Wilhelm, J. D. (2014). The role visualization strategies play in struggling readers' engagement, comprehension, and response to text or "Wait. You mean it's supposed to make sense every time you read?" In J. Flood, S. B. Heath & D. Lapp (Eds.), *The handbook of research on teaching literacy through the communicative and visual arts* (Vol. 2, pp. 413–422). New York, NY: Taylor & Francis.

McGee, L. M. (1992). Focus on research: Exploring the literature-based reading revolution. *Language Arts, 69*(7), 529–537.

Merleau-Ponty, M. (1962). *Phenomenology of perception: An introduction*. London, England: Routledge.

Moroye, C. M. & Uhrmacher, P. B. (2012). Standards, not standardization: Orchestrating aesthetic educational experiences. *Language Arts Journal of Michigan, 28*(1), 65–69.

Nayar, P. K. (2014). *Posthumanism*. Cambridge, England: Polity.

Muth, W. (2016). "A big circle of unity": Incarcerated fathers being-in-text. *Journal of Literacy Research, 48*(3), 317–345.

Nixon, H. & Comber, B. (2001). Books for adolescents: Film and video bridge popular and classroom cultures. *Journal of Adolescent & Adult Literacy, 44*(5), 480–487.

Nussbaum, M. C. (1998). The narrative imagination. In N. C. Nussbaum (Ed.), *Cultivating humanity: A classical defense of reform in liberal education* (pp. 85–112). Cambridge, MA: Harvard University Press.

Pahl, K. (2014). *Materializing literacies in communities: The uses of literacy revisited*. London, England: Bloomsbury.

Pahl, K. & Rowsell, J. with Collier, D., Pool, S., Rasool, Z., & Trzecak, T. (2020). *Living literacies*. Boston, MA: MIT Press.

Parsons, J. & Taylor, L. (2011). *Student engagement: What do we know and what should we do?* Report conducted by the University of Alberta for University Partners. 59 pp.

Parsons, L. T. (2006). Visualizing worlds from words on a page. *Language Arts, 83*(6), 492–500.

Parsons, M. (2002). Aesthetic experience and the construction of meanings. *Journal of Aesthetic Education, 36*(2), 24–37.

Radstone, S. (2007). Trauma theory: Contexts, politics, ethics. *Paragraph, 30*(1), 9–29.

Reinking, D. (2001). Multimedia and engaged reading in a digital world. In L. Verhoeven & C. Snow (Eds.), *Literacy and motivation: Reading engagement in individuals and groups* (pp. 195–221). Mahwah, NJ: Lawrence Erlbaum Associates.

Ricoeur, P. (1981). *Hermeneutics and the human sciences: Essays on language, action and interpretation* (J. Thompson, Trans.). Cambridge, MA: Cambridge University Press, and Paris, France: Éditions de la Maison des Sciences de l'Homme.

Ricoeur, P. (1985). *Temps et récit III: Le temps raconté*. Paris, France: Seuil.

Ricoeur, P. (1990). *Soi-même comme un autre*. Paris, France: Seuil.

Rosenblatt, L. M. (1938/1976). *Literature as exploration*. New York, NY: Noble & Noble.

Rosenblatt, L. M. (1978). *The reader, the text, the poem: The transactional theory of the literary work*. Carbondale/Edwardsville: Southern Illinois University Press.

Roskos, K. & Neuman, S. B. (2014). Best practices in reading: A 21st century skill update. *The Reading Teacher*, *67*(7), 507–511.

Rowsell, J. (2013). *Working with multimodality: Rethinking literacy in a digital age*. London, England: Routledge.

Rowsell, J. (2014). Toward a phenomenology of contemporary reading. *Australian Journal of Language and Literacy*, *37*(2), 117–127.

Rowsell, J. & Kendrick, M. (2013). Boys' hidden literacies: The critical need for the visual. *Journal of Adolescent and Adult Literacy*, *56*(7), 587–599.

Rowsell, J., Lemieux, A., Swartz, L., Burkitt, J. & Turcotte, M. (2018). The stuff that heroes are made of: Elastic, sticky, messy literacies in children's transmedial cultures. *Language Arts*, *96*(1), 7–20.

Sameshima, P. (2019). Ma, I'm thinking about nothing. In P. Sameshima, B. White & A. Sinner (Eds.). Ma: Materiality in *t*eaching and *l*earning (pp. 3–16). New York, NY: Peter Lang.

Sarroub, L. K. & Pernicek, T. (2016). Boys, books, and boredom: A case of three high school boys and their encounters with literacy. *Reading & Writing Quarterly*, *32*(1), 27–55.

Schallert, D. L. & Reed, J. H. (1997). The pull of the text and the process of involvement in reading. *Reading engagement: Motivating readers through integrated instruction* (pp. 68–85). Newark, DE: International Reading Association.

Seel, M. (2008). On the scope of aesthetic experience. In R. Shusterman & A. Tomlin (Eds.), *Aesthetic experience* (Routledge Studies in Contemporary Philosophy, pp. 98–105). New York, NY/London, England: Routledge.

Shernoff, D. J., Csikszentmihalyi, M., Schneider, B. & Shernoff, E. S. (2003). Student engagement in high school classrooms from the perspective of flow theory. *School Psychology Quarterly*, *18*(2), 158–176.

Shusterman, R. (2008). Aesthetic experience: From analysis to Eros. In R. Shusterman & A. Tomlin (Eds.), *Aesthetic experience* (pp. 79–97). New York, NY: Routledge.

Sousanis, N. (2015). *Unflattening*. Cambridge, MA: Harvard University Press.

St. Clair, R. (2005). Similarity and superunknowns: An essay on the challenges of educational research. *Harvard Educational Review*, *75*(4), 435–453.

Stanovich, K. (1986). Matthew effects in reading: Some consequences of individual differences in the acquisition of literacy. *Journal of Adolescent and Adult Literacy*, *47*, 454–461.

Stornaiuolo, A. & Whitney, E. H. (2018). Writing as worldmaking. *Language Arts*, *95*(4), 205–217.

Sullivan, A. & Brown, M. (2015). Reading for pleasure and progress in vocabulary and mathematics. *British Educational Research Journal*, *41*(6), 971–991.s

Sumara, D. J., Luce-Kapler, R. & Iftody, T. (2008). Educating consciousness through literary experiences. *Educational Philosophy and Theory*, *40*(1), 228–241.

Thomas, E. E. & Stornaiuolo, A. (2016). Restorying the self: Bending toward textual justice. *Harvard Educational Review*, *86*(3), 313–338.

Uhrmacher, P. B. (2009). Toward a theory of aesthetic learning experiences. *Curriculum Inquiry*. *39*(5), 613–636.

Van Manen, M. (1990). *Researching lived experience: Human science for an action sensitive pedagogy*. London, ON: Althouse Press.

Van Manen, M. (2002). Writing in the dark. In M. Van Manen (Ed.), *Writing in the dark: Phenomenological studies in interpretive inquiry* (pp. 237–252). London, ON: Althouse Press.

Van Manen, M. (2014). *Phenomenology of practice: Meaning-giving methods in phenomenological research and writing*. Walnut Creek, CA: Left Coast Press.

White, B. (1998). Aesthetigrams: Mapping aesthetic experiences. *Studies in Art Education*, *39*(40), 321–335.

White, B. (2007). Aesthetic encounters: Contributions to teacher education. *International Journal of Education & the Arts*, *8*(17), 1–28.

White, B. (2011). Private perceptions, public reflections: Aesthetic encounters as vehicles for shared meaning making. *International Journal of Education & the Arts*, *12*(LAI 2), 1–26.

White, B. (2013). Pay attention, pay attention, pay attention. In B. White & T. Costantino (Eds.), *Aesthetics, empathy and education* (pp. 99–116). New York, NY: Peter Lang.

White, B. & Lemieux, A. (2017). *Mapping holistic learning: An introductory guide to aesthetigrams*. New York, NY: Peter Lang.

White, B. & Tompkins, S. (2005). Doing aesthetics to facilitate meaning-making. *Arts and Learning Research Journal*, *21*(1), 1–36.

Wigfield, A. (1997). Children's motivations for reading and reading engagement. In J. T. Guthrie & A. Wigfield (Eds.), *Reading engagement: Motivating readers through integrated instruction* (pp. 14–33). Newark, DE: International Reading Association.

Wigfield, A. & Guthrie, J. T. (1997). Relations of children's motivation for reading to the amount and breadth of their reading. *Journal of Educational Psychology*, *89*, 420–432.

Wigfield, A., Guthrie, J. T., Perencevich, K. C., Taboada, A., Klauda, S. L., McRae, A. & Barbosa, P. (2008). Role of reading engagement in mediating effect of reading comprehension instruction on reading outcomes. *Psychology in the Schools*, *45*(5), 432–445.

Wittgenstein, L. (1953). *Philosophical investigations*. New York, NY: Macmillan.

Zahavi, D. (2016). *Self & other: Exploring subjectivity, empathy, and shame*. Oxford, England: Oxford University Press.

Zembylas, M. (2015). *Emotion and trauma conflict: Reclaiming healing in education*. Oxford, England: Oxford University Press.

CHAPTER THREE

Illustrating Reading Engagement: Indicators, Meaning-Making, and Beyond

In previous chapters, I described how reading engagement can be understood and delineated through such epistemologies and frameworks as phenomenological hermeneutics and posthumanism. I find that context and governmental initiatives can help frame the larger scope of the work being done on reading engagement, regardless of the epistemologies used. Finding ways to foster and improve reading engagement in adolescents has been a subject of international governmental concern in the past few decades, and the Canadian educational system is no exception. Reading for pleasure has been at the core of important educational discussions that direct tangents and influence decisions at the curriculum level. Sponsored by the Canadian Commission for UNESCO, the Canadian National Reading Campaign—which brings together readers, educators, librarians, parents, and publishers with the aim of making reading a national priority—regularly conducts Pleasure Reading Surveys and mandates reports on reading engagement. A key finding in recent years has been that in Ontario, 50% of third-graders reported that they liked to read in 2010–2011, which was a 26% drop compared to the 1998–1999 school year where 76% reported reading for pleasure (People for Education/PfE, 2011). The same study maintained that sixth-graders who enjoyed reading fell from 65% to 50% in the same period. The issue was raised in other countries like England, where it has been found that there should be immediate attention brought to reader engagement and the promotion of reading for pleasure in educational contexts (Cremin, 2014).

In a recent issue of *Literacy* on assessment, accountability, and policy, Moss (2017) emphasized the importance of considering variations in teaching and evaluating children's work, especially in light of the increase in standardized, number-driven tests in England. Standardization can only do so much for education (Moss, 2017), and in this line of thought Canadian researchers have also specified that test scores cannot be the sole determinant for measuring engagement (People for Education, 2011). The problem is not so much what standardization *does*, it is how standardization does *what it* does; and I maintain that while traditional testing methods and standardization can be useful for some purposes, other methods, such as mapping, can be used to bolster reading engagement in a holistic manner.

Boys' Reading Engagement: PISA Results and the Status Quo in Canada

Several Canadian researchers have pointed to the need to unveil boys' hidden literacies (Brozo, 2010; Rowsell & Kendrick, 2013), especially since it is commonly conveyed that boys tend to struggle more as readers than girls (Cremin, 2007, 2014; Moss, 2007). In the 2010 OECD PISA survey, one of the main reported issues was that boys were less engaged in reading than girls in more than 30 countries, including England (Cremin, 2014) and Canada (Klinger, Shulha & Wade-Woolley, 2009; White, 2007). Five years later in the 2015 OECD PISA study, the Canadian statistics remained unchanged: Canadian girls still outperformed boys in reading (CMEC, 2016). These results crystallized the international tendency that across OECD countries boys had lower scores than girls in reading by 27 points in PISA 2015. In Canada, the gender gap in scores rose to 26 points (CMEC, 2016), which was close to the international average. In light of the gender discrepancies in reading engagement scores, more attention should be paid to alternative ways of investigating reading engagement (Cremin, 2007, 2014).

In this chapter, I explore Canadian high school boys' reading engagement patterns as they respond to narratives using a mapping strategy that has proven to enhance engagement in previous studies (Lemieux, 2015, 2016; White, 2013). As described in earlier chapters, aesthetigram-making is a strategy embedded in phenomenological inquiry (Van Manen, 1990, 2014) and draws on the transactional theory of reading (Rosenblatt, 1978) in that it seeks to explore the phenomena emerging from the reciprocal and relational spaces between the reader and the read object. Aesthetigram-making investigates the aesthetic perspectives, embodiment, and emotions felt by students (Rowsell & Collier, 2016). This is of importance because, as Cremin (2014) points out, "the experience of reading literature and the deep emotional engagement which can be engendered needs to be more fully acknowledged and explicitly valued as a palpable benefit of independent reading" (p. 10). In the same line of thought, this chapter acknowledges the affective engagement that arises during reading transactions.

Re/framing Reading Engagement: When Phenomenology Comes In

Reading engagement, both as a term and concept, has generated multiple debates and nourished polemics in recent years. Contributing to these discussions, Cremin (2014) provided a useful review of the literature outlining how cognitive-oriented researchers have historically framed reading engagement as a subdivision of reading motivation, comprehension, and attainment[8]. Although researchers and policymakers still need access to further research framing reading engagement as a phenomenological manifestation of student engagement with read works, 'engagement' can be understood through plural, simultaneous manifestations of student expressions. Using a grounded theory framework where indicators of reading engagement are defined, students' responses are rated as engaged when they correspond to the indicators and criteria I developed in the analysis, which I explain in the "Indicators of Reading Engagement" section.

Reading stances are not antagonistically informed, they are plural and relational (Barthes, 1973, p. 52). Thus, aesthetigram-making in literature classes is epistemologically based on the understanding that phenomenological accounts always precede any hermeneutical mediation (Ricoeur, 1981, 1992; Van Manen, 1990, 2014). The aesthetigram strategy is a heuristic tool designed to examine traces of adolescents' reading engagement with literary works (novels, plays, short stories, poems) they are required to read for school. In previous studies (Lemieux, 2017; White & Lemieux, 2017), I showed how the strategy helped students (1) develop self-confidence in their interactions with literary works through aesthetically inspired meaning-making, and (2) heighten their reflection on their personal values as they develop responses to literary works. Mapping is thus understood and conceived as a participative and agentic tool.

8. See, for example, the important contributions of reading researchers Jamie Metsala, John Guthrie, and Allan Wigfield, and their work on Concept-Oriented Reading Instruction (CORI).

Indicators of Reading Engagement

In this chapter, I analyze the qualitative results of the previously described study with indicators of reading engagement to provide examples of how reading engagement can be studied, in part, through concrete, defined indicators. These should be read as partial and take into account the posthuman and more-than-human ethos of texts being read and the readers themselves. To design the former framework, I read and analyzed a body of scientific literature detailing qualitative instances of reading engagement; from there I developed and compiled seven indicators of reading engagement. That is, when a reader is engaged, he:

1. Develops his fantasmical activity (Langlade, 2006; see also Lewkowich, 2015, 2016a, 2016b on reading as desire) whereby the reader adds, suppresses, or modifies plot events to orchestrate the story he would like to read or see happening.
2. Experiences instances of mimetic coherence (Langlade, 2006), whereby the reader completes the narrative by making links between events (these links and relationships are not visible in the original narrative; for example: Character A avenged Character B because Character B always protected Character A—but the reader has no concrete evidence of this documented protection because it comes from the reader's imagination).
3. Undergoes instances of visual realization (see also Brehm, 2011; Rowsell, 2013; Rowsell & Kendrick, 2013), whereby the reader personally experiences sensory reactions (e.g., he will be reminded of certain sounds, smells, or will perceive the action in a way that is associated with images that manifest in the reader's mind).
4. Exercises his axiological judgment (Langlade, 2006). That is, the reader will judge characters based on his decisions or moral values, (e.g., "I think Character A was selfish in asking for Character B's help").
5. Encounters levels of malaise, confusion, and/or surprise with regards to a situation he has read (Langlade, 2015).
6. Realises the aesthetic impact of texts (Lacelle & Langlade, 2008) by identifying how the text's form, format, style, sidebars, glossaries, indexes, and layout can affectively influence a reader's understanding of a text.
7. Feels empathy toward characters (Bogdan, 1992; Ivey & Johnston, 2013; Lysaker & Miller, 2012; Muth, 2016; Nussbaum, 1998; White, 2011).

Aesthetigrams as Research and Teaching Tools

Aesthetigrams were first designed as teaching tools in a study White (1998) conducted in an undergraduate class on aesthetics, where he provided students with a concrete strategy to record moment-by-moment responses to visual artworks. The strategy has since expanded (White, 2007, 2011, 2014; White & Tompkins, 2005) into a self-exploratory tool with two purposes: (1) to provide a framework for the writing of experiential art criticism; and (2) to contribute to ongoing research into the nature of aesthetic experiences. Aesthetigrams are phenomenologically grounded maps that describe the moment-by-moment lived experiences and reactions of humans reading, making, viewing, and interacting with artworks. They are also hermeneutic in their spontaneous interpretations of events. They partake in posthumanist thought insofar as they engage map-makers in an awareness of what takes place affectively and cognitively as they react to multimodal and monomodal works.

I previously used aesthetigrams in a study of senior high school students' engagement patterns with text and film narratives (Lemieux, 2016). The latter results pointed to differing engagement patterns (such as expectations and affective states) as students watched the adapted film version of the written narrative. In this chapter, my focus will be adolescents' reading engagement patterns as they read the written narrative, all the while showing a case study of a participant's reactions to the film version. The objective of this procedure is to demonstrate how aesthetigrams can be used both as teaching and research tools in applied settings. To explain the history of this protocol, I review in this section five studies that featured White's aesthetigrams as both teaching and research tools.

Based on Jones's (1979) model of aesthetic balance which highlights different emphases in response patterns, White and Tompkins (2005) described the use and necessity of keeping track of students' reactions to artworks in developing awareness of aesthetic encounters. These encounters provide a snapshot of the layers of experience embedded in the self. The visual mapping further allowed the researchers to examine the materialized and represented patterns of student perceptions with regards to the objects they contemplated.

Concurrently, White (2007) showed that aesthetigrams could serve as self-learning tools for students, and guide educator-researchers in their teaching. White (2011) pursued the concept of self-learning in a case study of four adult participants who responded to thought-provoking visual artworks, and provided detailed commentary and ekphrastic poetry as extensions of their perceptual experiences. Qualitative data pointed to the articulation of values as expressed in participants' meaning-making strategies. The data provided valuable, specialized insights into the breadth of experiences one can undergo, all the while emphasizing that each experience is situational, personal, unpredictable, and perceptual. White's articles showcase the potential for teachers to guide students in navigating their interactions with artworks, and to the variable nature of those aesthetically oriented interactions.

In *Student Generated Art Criticism*, White (2014) reported on the findings of a qualitative case study outlining the experiences of three pre-service teachers enrolled in an elective undergraduate class. Building on his previous research on aesthetigrams, White discovered that the strategy helped participants mobilize awareness of empathetic skills. That is, students who demonstrated such awareness had empathy as part of their personal values. These studies provided support for the direction of this chapter and other work (see Lemieux, 2016; White & Lemieux, 2017). Moreover, these projects demonstrated that individual reactions to artworks (including literature and film) are felt and embodied. Furthermore, they showed that moment-by-moment responses to artworks can be researched, and those moments provided insights into features of student engagement.

I recently did a study (Lemieux, 2017) highlighting how aesthetigrams could be used as teaching and research tools when exploring female high school students' reactions to literature. As such, I developed a condensed typology based on White's (2011) experiential categories, which were used by participants to chart their moment-by-moment interactions with texts. Here, I build on White's (2011) study and expand on previous results and categories (Lemieux, 2015, 2017), adapting them for high school students to record their experiential moments in response to films and narratives.

Methodology

This recent study took place in a mixed private high school of the Greater Montreal Area and was conducted over six weeks in the context of a literature class. I worked with 88 adolescents who used aesthetigrams to visually represent traces of their reading engagement patterns. In this chapter, I show an example of an adolescent boy who partook in the study. Participants were high school students enrolled in grade 11, and the research was conducted during regular class hours. The school programmes students were enrolled in ranged from sports to media and technology, and literature was a core course for all students.

Students experienced aesthetigram-making and its related agentic coding procedures in their literature classroom. The first day of the project, I introduced students to the aesthetigram strategy by doing a PowerPoint presentation and showing them a step-by-step, moment-by-moment making process. The methodological procedure prepared students to:

1. List their reactions to a book excerpt (from the play *Incendies*).
2. Rank these reactions by assessing their importance (e.g., Was it a fleeting moment or a more discernible moment?).
3. Associate them to a category of their choice, as detailed in a glossary of reactions (White, 1998, 2013).
4. Color code these reactions.
5. Arrange the coded responses on a map.

Students repeated the same procedure in response to the corresponding scene of the movie. I used the aforementioned reading engagement indicators to examine the nature of participants' engagement patterns in response to the book and film.

Summary of the Narrative

Students read one of the final scenes of *Incendies* (2003), a play written by Wajdi Mouawad. The scene ("Letter to the Son") presents a letter written by a woman who was once a prisoner. This letter is addressed to her biological son, and expresses that she forgives him for what he did to her. (He raped her when he was working as a prison guard, not knowing she was his mother). In this poignant and controversial scene, she manifests forgiveness and compassion for him.

Analysis

Artifactual and qualitative data are crucial to this study. The following maps provide concrete examples of an adolescent's engagement patterns. For the purposes of this chapter, I present a case study highlighting one reader's foci and response tendencies, in order to show ways of working with subjective response and evaluation in the literature classroom. This procedure has been used by Pantaleo (2013) to showcase reading engagement patterns in a case study. I then provide qualitative charts retracing data from the larger study through eleven analyzed maps, with the aim of showing the varying response emphases and richness of reading engagement in participants.

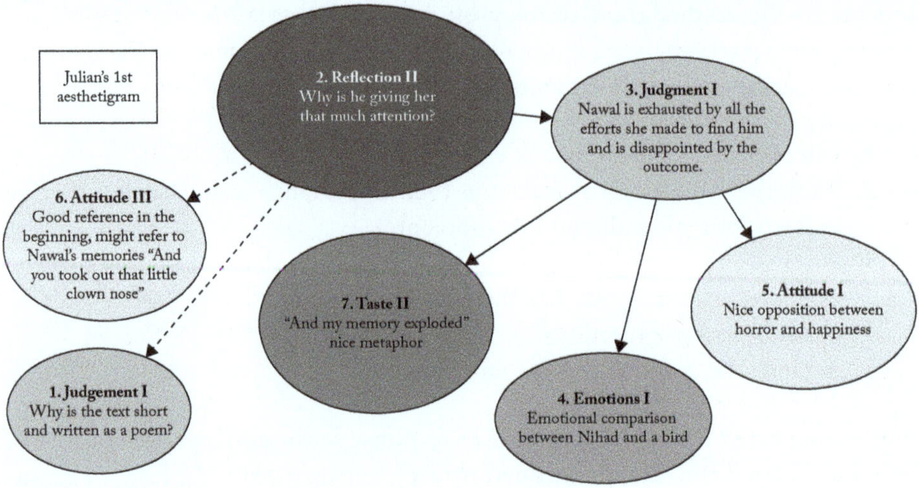

Figure 6: Julian's first aesthetigram, in response to the book excerpt.

Mapping Reactions to Text

Julian's accompanying commentary: Since my second reaction (Reflection II) is the most important one, I placed it above all others. Then, I placed reaction 3 (Judgment I) closer to the second reaction, because it amplified and justified why I am asking myself this question in the second reaction. Then, reactions 4, 5, and 7 are situated beneath reaction 3 because they all justify and amplify my third reaction. Finally, reactions 1 and 6 are placed a bit further because they were less relevant.

Julian's aesthetigram lays out situated evidence through his traces of reading engagement. Analyzing his map and accompanying commentary, Julian stated that his most important reaction was his third one, where he described his perceived impression of Nawal's exhaustion and deception. The narrative does not explicitly point to these felt emotions. This moment, placed in the Judgment category, exemplifies how a reader, Julian in this case, experiences a degree of fantasmical activity. That is, Julian deems that the mother is exasperated even though he does not have concrete evidence of this, and so he alters the narrative—based on his axiological judgment (she is disappointed)—towards the mother. These observations are traces of reading engagement experienced by the reader.

Julian explained how his reactions #4, #5, and #7 emerged from his third moment. Reaction #4, which he placed in the Emotions category, described his comparing Nihad to a bird. This reaction reflects aesthetic impact because Julian qualified the comparison as emotional; the stylistic attributes of the text have an impact on the reader's affect, and serve as an indicator of reading engagement (aesthetic impact). Julian wrote in his fifth reaction that there was a nice opposition or tension between happiness and horror, which is another indicator of aesthetic impact. That is, Julian's observation on the style of the text, and the felt expression that this stylistic choice is pleasant, is a sign of reading engagement. The same observation can be made for his seventh reaction, where he notes another positive metaphor and places it in the taste category, where it is a question of aesthetic impact. In other words, Julian's reading of the style and format impacted his aesthetic view of the text in a way he qualified as pleasant. He placed his second reaction ("why is he giving her that much attention?") in the Reflection category. This reaction points to an indicator of reading engagement, insofar as Julian reflected on a question that triggered his axiological judgment. In other words, the question he formulated has judgment undertones that imply a certain level of reading engagement.

Julian designed two additional reactions (#1 and #6) that he linked using dashed arrows, explaining that these moments were less relevant than his other ones. Reaction #1 was placed in the Judgment category and pointed to a question or a reflection towards an observation of form and a trace of aesthetic impact. Reaction #6 described a situation that highlights Julian's reflection on the mother's memories: "Good reference in the beginning, might refer to Nawal's memories." This is an example where Julian activated his mimetic coherence by trying to complete the narrative and venture suppositions.

In summary, Julian designed and placed seven reactions in his first aesthetigram. These reactions, placed in five different categories (Attitude, Reflection, Judgment, Taste, and Emotion) reflect the following indicators of reading engagement: aesthetic impact, mimetic coherence, axiological judgment, and fantasmical activity.

Julian's accompanying commentary: I decided to organize my reactions in a hierarchy. I put in the first level the most intense reaction that I felt, and the less intense reaction in the third level.

Julian's second aesthetigram is organized methodically and meticulously, as is explained in his accompanying commentary. His most important reaction was his fourth one, which he placed at the top of his map. Placed in the Attitude category, his fourth response described his dislike towards the lack of visual evidence in the mother's reaction when the son opened the letter she wrote to him, a critical point in the plot, and emphasized in the written version. During this scene in the film adaptation, the mother's voice can be heard (voiceover as monologue). However, her face remains unseen, and the camera is oriented towards a white wall instead. Julian's dissatisfaction with this scene is an instance of aesthetic impact because of

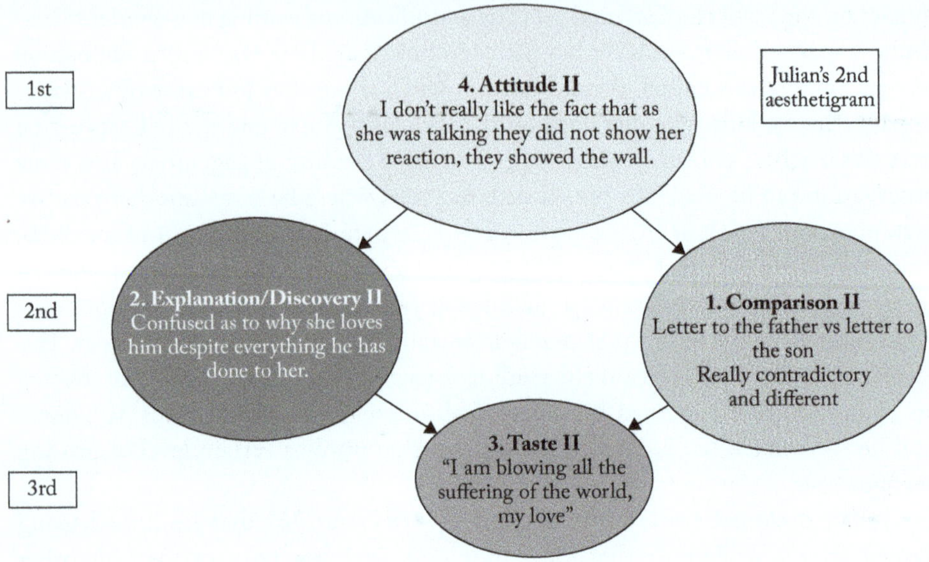

Figure 7: Julian's second aesthetigram, in response to the corresponding film excerpt.

his observations on how camera angles and shots can influence and manipulate a viewer's affective reception.

In the second level of his map, Julian placed two reactions (#1 and #2). Reaction 1 is a comparison that juxtaposes the contradictions and differences between "Letter to the Son" and another scene ("Letter to the Father"). Julian's awareness level—notably the fact that he acknowledges such differences—is an example of axiological judgment since the reader qualifies the letters with attributes that are positive judgments. His opinion, expressed through these words, marks a degree of engagement that can be identified through axiological judgment. In addition, Julian's second reaction is one of malaise and confusion and echoes the corresponding category of reading engagement. A student's confusion towards a narrative is an indicator of engagement because it is through these confrontations that readers become aware and engaged, as living beings who ontologically develop in time (Abram, 1996).

Finally, Julian's third reaction pointed to an appreciation of a specific line of the film. This preference indicates that Julian was engaging with this sentence at a given time, and provides evidence of engagement insofar as the film influenced his affective reactions and reception of the piece (aesthetic impact). In total, Julian's second aesthetigram was comprised of four reactions spread over four categories. These reactions show evidence of engagement through three themes: aesthetic impact, confusion/malaise, and axiological judgment. In the following chapter,

I present the maps of adolescent boys who also partook in the larger study, and provide charts that point to emphases in response. These aesthetigrams provide further details as to how to use the strategy in pedagogical and research settings.

References

Abram, D. (1997). *The spell of the sensuous: Perception and language in a more-than-human world.* New York, NY: Vintage Books.

Barthes, R. (1973). *Le plaisir du texte.* Paris, France: Seuil.

Bogdan, D. (1992). *Re-education the imagination: Towards a poetics, politics, and pedagogy of literary engagement.* Portsmouth, NH: Heinemann.

Brehm, S. (2011). Du sens aux sens: Les représentations mentales dans l'acte de lecture. *Protée, 39*(2), 107–112.

Brozo, W. G. (2010). *To be a boy, to be a reader: Engaging teen and preteen boys in active literacy* (2nd ed.). Newark, DE: International Reading Association.

CMEC/Council of Ministers of Education, Canada. (2016). *Measuring up: Canadian results of the OECD PISA Study: The performance of Canada's youth in science, reading and mathematics. 2015 first results for Canadians aged 15.* Toronto, ON: Council of Ministers of Education, Canada.

Cremin, T. (2007). Revisiting reading for pleasure: Diversity, delight and desire. In K. Goouch & A. Lambirth (Eds.), *Understanding phonics and the teaching of reading* (pp. 166–190). Berkshire, England: McGraw-Hill.

Cremin, T. (2014). Reading for pleasure and reader engagement: Reviewing the research. In T. Cremin, M. Mottram, S. Powell, R. Collins & K. Safford (Eds.), *Building communities of engaged readers: Reading for pleasure* (pp. 5–19). London, England: Routledge.

Ivey, G. & Johnson, P. H. (2013). Engagement with young adult literature: Outcomes and processes. *Reading Research Quarterly, 48*(3), 255–275.

Jones, R. L. Jr. (1979). Phenomenological balance and aesthetic response. *Journal of Aesthetic Education, 13*(1), 93–106.

Klinger, D. A., Shulha, L. A. & Wade-Woolley, L. (2009). *Towards an understanding of gender differences in literacy achievement.* Toronto, ON: Government of Ontario, Education Quality and Accountability Office.

Lacelle, N. & Langlade, G. (2008). Former des lecteurs/spectateurs par la lecture subjective des œuvres. In J.-L. Dufays (Ed.), *Enseigner et apprendre la littérature aujourd'hui pour quoi faire?* (pp. 55–65). Louvain-la-Neuve, France: Presses Universitaires de Louvain.

Langlade, G. (2006). L'activité fictionnalisante du lecteur. In M. Braud, B. Laville & B. Louichon (Eds.), *Les enseignements de la fiction* (pp. 163–176). Bordeaux, France: Presses de l'Université de Bordeaux.

Langlade, G. (2015). Événement de lecture et avènement du lecteur. In M. Cambron & G. Langlade (Eds.), *L'événement de lecture* (pp. 39–57). Québec, QC: Nota Bene.

Lemieux, A. (2015). Think it through: Fostering aesthetic experiences to raise interest in literature at the high school level. *Journal of the Canadian Association for Curriculum Studies, 12*(2), 66–93.

Lemieux, A. (2016). Moments de réception en lecture et en spectature : Le cas d'Incendies au CEGEP. *Revue de recherches en littératie médiatique multimodale (R2LMM), 3*(November, Special Issue, "Digital writing in schools: New textualities, new outcomes").

Lemieux, A. (2017). Recent developments: Aesthetigram-making in the literature classroom. In B. White & A. Lemieux (Eds.), *Mapping Holistic Learning: An introductory guide to aesthetigrams* (pp. 73–100). New York, NY: Peter Lang.

Lewkowich, D. (2015). Transferences of teacher-casting and projections of redemptions: Teacher education, young adult literature and the psychic life of reading. *Pedagogy, Culture & Society, 23*(3), 349–368.

Lewkowich, D. (2016a). To enter the text as into a dream: Tracing the unconscious effects of reading experience. *International Journal of Research & Method in Education, 39*(1), 58–73.

Lewkowich, D. (2016b). The reader's read and the dreamer's dream: Fringing the unconscious. In G. Reis, A. Ibrahim & N. Ng-A-Fook (Eds.), *Provoking curriculum studies: Strong poetry and arts of the possible in education* (pp. 161–172). New York, NY: Routledge.

Lysaker, J. T. & Miller, A. (2012). Engaging social imagination: The developmental work of wordless book reading. *Journal of Early Childhood Literacy, 13*(2), 147–174.

Moss, G. (2007). *Literacy and gender: Researching texts, contexts and readers.* New York, NY: Routledge.

Moss, G. (2017). Assessment, accountability and the literacy curriculum: Reimagining the future in the light of the past. *Literacy, 51*(2), 56–64.

Mouawad, W. (2003). *Incendies.* Montréal, QC: Leméac.

Muth, W. (2016). "A big circle of unity": Incarcerated fathers being-in-text. *Journal of Literacy Research, 48*(3), 317–345.

Nussbaum, M. C. (1998). *Cultivating humanity: A classical defense of reform in liberal education.* Cambridge, MA: Harvard University Press.

Pantaleo, S. (2013). Revisiting Rosenblatt's aesthetic response through *The Arrival. Australian Journal of Language and Literacy, 36*(3), 125–134.

People for Education/PfE. (2011). *Reading for joy.* Ontario Education Quality and Accountability Office (EQAO). Retrieved from http://www.peopleforeducation.ca/document/reading-for-joy

Ricoeur, P. (1981). *Hermeneutics and the human sciences: Essays on language, action and interpretation* (J. Thompson, Trans.). Cambridge, MA: Cambridge University Press, and Paris, France: Éditions de la Maison des Sciences de l'Homme.

Ricoeur, P. (1992). *Oneself as another.* Chicago, IL: Chicago University Press.

Rosenblatt, L. M. (1978). *The reader, the text, the poem: The transactional theory of the literary work.* Carbondale/Edwardsville: Southern Illinois University Press.

Rowsell, J. (2013). *Working with multimodality: Rethinking literacy in a digital age.* London, England: Routledge.

Rowsell, J. & Collier, D. (2016). Researching multimodality in language and education. In K. King, Y.-J. Lai & S. May (Eds.), *Encyclopedia of language and education* (pp. 1–14). Cham, Switzerland: Springer.

Rowsell, J. & Kendrick, M. (2013). Boys' hidden literacies: The critical need for the visual. *Journal of Adolescent and Adult Literacy, 56*(7), 587–599.

Van Manen, M. (1990). *Researching lived experience: Human science for an action sensitive pedagogy*. London, ON: Althouse Press.

Van Manen, M. (2014). *Phenomenology of practice: Meaning-giving methods in phenomenological research and writing*. Walnut Creek, CA: Left Coast Press.

White, B. (1998). Aesthetigrams: Mapping aesthetic experiences. *Studies in Art Education, 39*(40), 321–335.

White, B. (2007). Aesthetic encounters: Contributions to teacher education. *International Journal of Education & the Arts, 8*(17), 1–28.

White, B. (2011). Private perceptions, public reflections: Aesthetic encounters as vehicles for shared meaning making. *International Journal of Education & the Arts, 12*(LAI 2), 1–26.

White, B. (2013). Pay attention, pay attention, pay attention. In B. White & T. Costantino (Eds.), *Aesthetics, empathy and education* (pp. 99–116). New York, NY: Peter Lang.

White, B. (2014). Student generated art criticism. *Canadian Review of Art Education, 41*(1), 32–55.

White, B. & Lemieux, A. (2017). *Mapping holistic learning: An introductory guide to aesthetigrams.* New York, NY: Peter Lang.

White, B. & Tompkins, S. (2005). Doing aesthetics to facilitate meaning-making. *Arts and Learning Research Journal, 21*(1), 1–36.

White, B. [Bozena]. (2007). Are girls better readers than boys? Which boys? Which girls? *Canadian Journal of Education, 30*(2), 554–581.

CHAPTER FOUR

Mapping Reactions across Students: Engagement Tendencies

In Chapter Three, I described indicators of reading engagement to look as traces of engagement in adolescents' mapped reactions. Then, I analyzed Julian's maps using those indicators and explained how mapping can be useful in research and pedagogical contexts. In this chapter, I present the maps of Tom, Oliver, Simon, Justin, Noah, Josh, Max, and Billy—eight adolescents who, like Julian, mapped their moment-by-moment reactions to the *Letter to the Son*. For Billy's case, I present both his aesthetigrams (one in response to the scene of the play, the second in response to the same scene in the film) as well as drawings he made to represent characters and provide an alternative book cover. Drawings have long been used in research (Afonso, 2004; Mitchell, 2011) to provide additional insights into phenomena; insights that words cannot always provide.

Tom's Accompanying Commentary

I placed the most important reaction in the middle. It represented the discovery of the reason why Nawal stayed silent. Then, I put my [expectations] reaction next to it because she is living a lot of emotions, which compel her to remain silent. I linked the two [former reactions] because they are the most important. My two judgments are relatively close to the center but they are not the most important

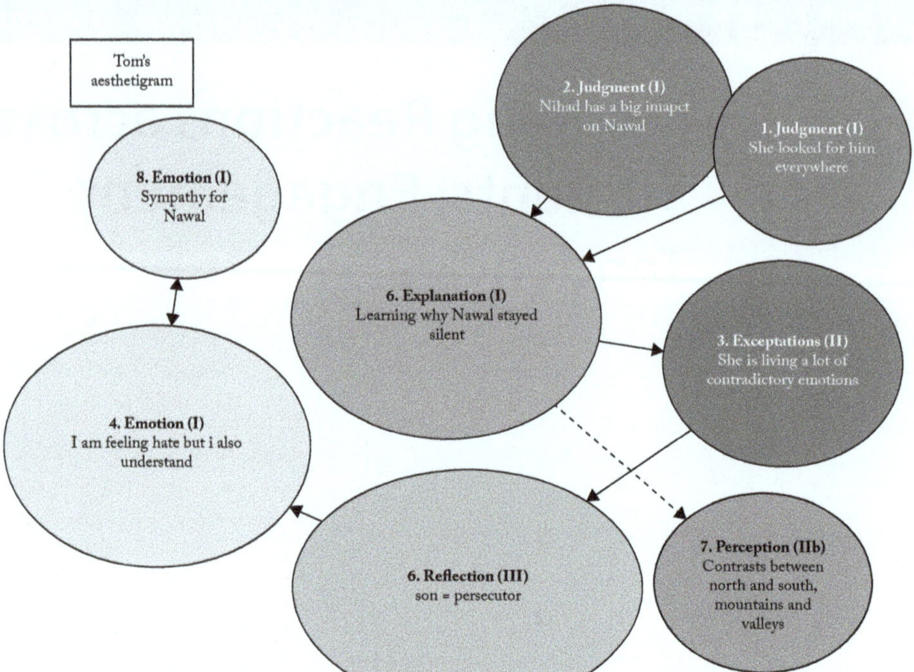

Figure 8: Tom's aesthetigram in response to Scene 37 in the play *Incendies*.

because they are kind of superficial. Finally, my emotions that I lived have a direct link with the centre and the fact that the son is also the persecutor.

An Analysis of Tom's Traces of Reading Engagement

Tom's commentary points to detailed and substantial traces of engagement. He indicated that his most important response took place when he learned why the mother, Nawal, wrote that she remained silent in that scene of the play. He categorized this response as "Explanation (I)" (the text is seen like a puzzle, a sign to decode or a problem to solve; it is essentially a positive reaction). Tom did express, in his sixth and third responses, that human responses to events are complex and sometimes result in conflicting thoughts and emotions. Based on previous studies (Bogdan, 1992; Brett, 2016; Larrivé, 2015; Nussbaum, 1998; White, 2013, 2014), empathy counts as evidence of engagement. Furthermore, one may argue that the *awareness* of a character's complexity is a form of empathy, and therefore engagement. Tom's sixth and third reactions could be placed in the mimetic coherence indicator of engagement, for the reader in this case attempts to make meaning by filling in the gaps. Additionally, these reactions reflect axiological judgment; that is, a judgment towards a character's actions. Tom's third reaction is one where he explains Nawal's motives and empathizes with Nawal ("she is living a lot of contradictory emotions, which compel her to remain silent"). In this moment, Tom puts himself in Nawal's shoes, and suggests a causal relationship between her contradictory emotions and her silence. This supposition can only be made possible when the reader can empathetically imagine himself as the narrator to justify or make sense of events. As Larrivé (2015) declares:

> Once the reader is mentally positioned in a fictional universe, fictional characters thus become the subjects with whom he experiences empathy. To understand what a character thinks or believes, the reader projects himself into that character's situation and, once settled in its internal context (its being) and in its external context (its environment), the reader uses his body as an analytical tool to gather assessments from this situation. (p. 161, my translation)

The nature of the relationships established by Tom represents that of a discovery, and an expectation with regards to what he has already read. Tom's first and second reactions were categorized in Judgment—an area where reactions are spontaneous and initial—and the reader judges a character with a qualifier (adjective). In this case, our reader felt these interpretations were less important: "My two judgments are […] not the most important because they are kind of superficial." It could be argued that since they were less important for the participant, his engagement was less pronounced during these moments.

That said, his acknowledgement of the fact that his judgments were less significant than other moments—that is, his ability to make comparisons—indicates a form of reflective state as a demonstration of post-encounter engagement. Even though he categorized them as judgments (which are, in this case, linked to mimetic coherence and axiological judgment), they were not prominent moments for him. Moreover, Tom noted that the reactions he placed in the Emotion (I) category (a sub-category of feelings, where one can associate a precise term/word, e.g., happiness, sadness, anger, shame, anxiety, etc.) were impactful insofar as he placed them near the center. This disposition is in line with the instructions I initially gave students to play with representation: the most impactful responses could be placed in the center of their aesthetigrams.

His eighth and fourth responses were placed in the Emotion category and indicated evidence of empathy for Nawal. In his eighth response, Tom noted "sympathy for Nawal," while in his fourth moment, he wrote, "I am feeling hate but I also understand." These responses are both in line with Larrivé's (2015) descriptions of empathy.

The fourth reaction was, however, more important for Tom than the eighth one, if we look at the size of the circles where each response was situated. Circle sizes were another representational cue I gave students to illustrate which moments were more impactful. For example, a large circle would point to an impactful moment, while a smaller circle would point to a more fleeting, difficult-to-discern type of moment. Tom further placed his response, "the son is also the persecutor," in Reflection (III), which is an investigation into formal qualities like structure and literary devices (e.g., wondering whether repetitions in the text have an impact on affect). Tom did not provide further explanations as to why he placed this response in this category, and he wrote that it was his sixth response (although there is already another sixth response). It is probable that this additional sixth response was a co-intended moment (assuming Tom did not make a mistake in his numbers), in line with the nature of human complexity. An awareness of this complexity is also a form of engagement as he reflects on his response patterns.

Interestingly, Tom has not provided commentary regarding his Perception (IIb) response (where *b* is a sub-category of Perception II), which is a descriptive moment or tendency to identify aspects of the narrative, with a subjective emphasis on preference regarding, in this case, form—scenery—contrasts between north and south, mountains and valleys. The absence of commentary, coupled with the fact that his reaction is placed within a small circle, are indicators that his attention in this regard was perhaps not as important to him. The awareness of this perception, however, shows the nature of his engagement as one of aesthetic impact.

Oliver's Accompanying Commentary

I decided to put in the center the reaction that felt like it was the most important. To me, it was that the text was deep. Then, on top, I put features of the letter that I noticed as I was reacting. They do not have a precise spot on my sheet I just decided to put them on top. Same thing goes for the bottom of the page, for my principal emotion. I put three "positives" (#8, #9, #5), that show how these were felt emotions during reading the letter. On the right, I placed moments that I liked personally and, to conclude, I put a statement on the left of my most important reaction that I noticed when I finished reading.

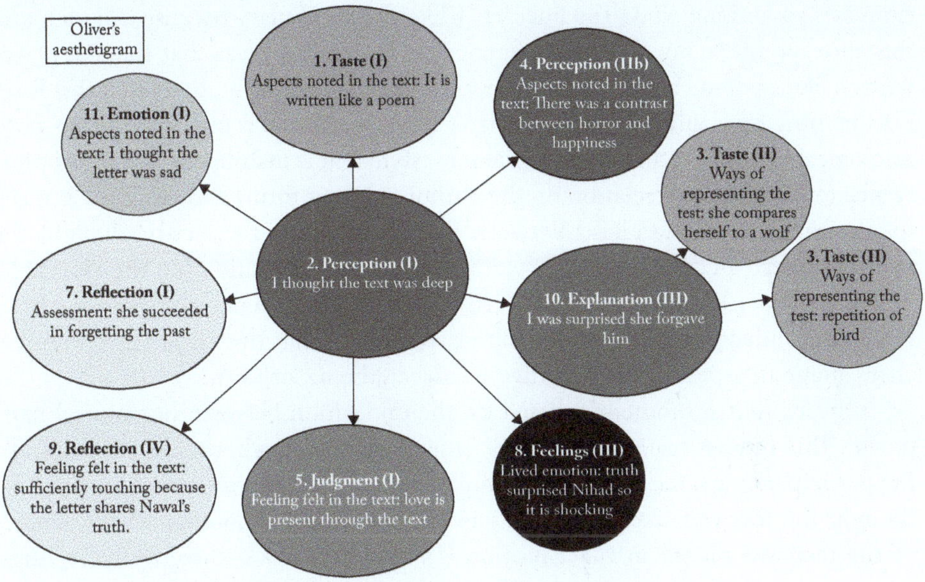

Figure 9: Oliver's aesthetigram in response to scene 37 in the play *Incendies*.

Analysis of Oliver's Traces of Reading Engagement

Oliver was one of the participants who recorded the most individual reactions to the written play, with eleven. There is much complexity in his map, which shows the depth and range of his reactions as some of them indicate traces of reading engagement. In his aesthetigram, Oliver noted three Taste moments (sub-categories I and II), two Perception moments (sub-categories I and IIb), two Reflection moments (sub-categories I and IV), and one moment of each of the following categories: Explanation (II), Emotion (I), Judgment (I), and Feelings (III).

Looking across reactions, Oliver's most important moment was his second one. He placed it in the center, and indicated that the "text was deep," which may reveal a felt emotion that triggered empathy, a moment coming from the participant's overall *gestalt* (White, 1998) towards the text. His other reactions all stemmed from this central one. Oliver explained that at the top of his aesthetigram, he put "features of the letter" that he jotted down as he was reading. He gave more detail in his map than in the accompanying commentary, and expressed that his three reactions placed on top of his map were based on "aspects of the text." He placed these reactions in three categories that is, Taste (I), Perception (IIb) and Emotion (I).

Oliver's first reaction was placed in the Taste (I) category, which is a general or known preference for certain types of literary forms or subjects (e.g., a remark that expresses something along the lines of "I like the vocabulary because it is rich and this corresponds to my general preferences"). His reaction was that the letter "was written like a poem," a fair observation, and his categorizing suggests that this form is something he would usually appreciate. This observation is one that reflects both axiological judgment (that is, a judgment on style that is manifested through a preference towards, or appreciation of, the author's chosen form) and aesthetic impact, for the participant made links between that reaction and the fact he thought the text was "deep." In comparison, Oliver placed his fourth reaction (on the aspects he noted in the text) in the Perception (IIb) category, that is, a descriptive moment or tendency to identify aspects of the narrative, with a subjective emphasis on preferences about an aspect of the narrative, a subject, theme, or form.

Oliver's fourth moment focused on the opposition between horror and happiness. This moment suggests reading engagement through aesthetic impact, for the participant's awareness of form is linked with his central reactions, in which he thought the text was "deep." The reader's third (eleventh) moment on the aspects of the text was placed in the Emotion (I) category (a sub-category of feelings, whereby one can associate a precise term/word, e.g., happiness, sadness, anger, shame, etc.), and described his thoughts on the letter ("I thought the letter was sad"). This is another example of the reader's felt emotions in relation to form, and shows traces of engagement in reading as a form of aesthetic impact. One of the contributions of Oliver's moments of engagement is his awareness of the text manifested in three distinct sites that all relate to the relationships between form and affect. Oliver's aesthetigram shows us that this "aesthetic impact" can therefore result from the accumulation of different student-generated meanings and placed categories. These meanings are not neutral or passive within maps, and give us insights into the participant's reading engagement patterns.

Oliver placed two repetitions (reactions #3 and #6) that were meaningful to him in the Taste (II) category, which is a subjective preference for an aspect of the narrative (e.g., "I like the description of the bird in the text"). He further explained that these two reactions were "ways of representing the text." There is a will on Oliver's part to be precise when describing form. Per the participant, moments #3 and #6 mirror the formal qualities of the text, and are also related to Lacelle and Langlade's (2007) "aesthetic impact" category. So far, the reactions noted are related to the participant's transaction with the formal qualities of the text, and are indicative of the types of engagement Oliver went through as he read scene 37. Then, Oliver's tenth reaction (placed in Explanation (II)) is connected to the fact that he "was surprised" when Nawal forgave her son. In addition to axiological judgment where the reader judges a character's action, this reaction speaks to Langlade's (2015) description of the reader's *surprise*—one of the conditions for reading engagement:

> Reading events always provoke surprise. They are the result of an unexpected meeting, submitted to the randomness of reading adventures. It thus happens through a break with reading expectations or predictable reactions, which is why we qualify it as a revelation. That reaction manifests the brutal and troublesome reaction of what we ignored, but that we immediately recognize as a part of the reader's identity and history. (my translation, p. 51)

Very structured, Oliver's aesthetigram contains a bottom part with three reactions he classified as the feelings and emotions he felt in his interactions with the text. In keeping with his organizational patterning procedure, he placed his reactions in three distinct categories: Reflection (IV), Judgment (I), and Feelings (III). Reflection IV is a category that points to the text's aesthetics. Indeed, Oliver's ninth reaction speaks to his "*feelings felt* in the text," which were "sufficiently *touching* because the letter shares Nawal's truth." This response reflects the fact that aesthetic form influences the participant's affect in terms of both aesthetic impact and empathy.

Oliver's fifth reaction was placed in Judgment (I), a category that embeds a spontaneous, initial reaction whereby the reader judges character Z to be exaggerating/happy/clumsy, etc. Oliver's "*felt feelings*" as he characterized them in reaction #5, described that "love is present through the text." It is possible that Oliver miscategorized his reaction, for "love" does not represent a judgment on a character as understood in the Judgment (I) category. Since mapping is a rhizomatic process that sometimes does not seek to elucidate, but rather inform, it is possible that the participant chose this category without further justification, and that is satisfactory as well. Despite lack of evidence as to why the participant categorized this reaction in Judgment (I), Oliver may have engaged with the text as a whole in a way that accentuates the thematic importance of love throughout the text. Since the participant added that it was a feeling derived from the text, we can thus refer to it as an indicator of empathy.

Oliver categorized his eighth reaction in Feelings (III), which is an affective orientation directed towards a generic expression in which the reader supposes that others will interpret (or should interpret) the work the same way that he does: "truth surprised Nihad, so it is shocking." Scene 37 indeed represents one of the climaxes of the play, in which the "truth" is revealed. It is a cathartic moment that was also shared by other readers in Oliver's class. Oliver's reaction can be categorized as a surprise moment of engagement (Langlade, 2015, p. 51). In addition, I argue that Oliver's reaction is one of fantasmical activity, for the text does not capture Nihad's embodied reaction. The participant completes the narrative by activating his own imaginary desire to complete the scene and fill in the gaps where comprehension might have been missed (mimetic coherence).

Oliver concludes his accompanying commentary by writing: "On the right, I placed moments that I liked personally and to conclude I put a statement on the left of my most important reaction that I noticed when I finished reading." The reaction he placed on the right of his aesthetigram was put in the Explanation (II) category (where the dominating reaction is one of frustration due to puzzlement or confusion, or a lack of access to the truth; it is essentially a negative reaction). It is detailed in the following statement: "I was surprised she forgave him" and speaks to Langlade's (2015) marker of engagement referring to a reader's "malaise" or "surprise" (p. 51). As in Billy's case, which we will see later in this chapter, puzzlement is also an indicator of reading engagement. We should note that there is no clear indication that Nawal concretely forgave her son (whether in the play or in the film). Instead, she wrote a letter, filled with love and hate as punctured tensions, and revealed that she was a victim of sexual assault perpetuated by her own son. Thus, Oliver drew on his fanstasmical activity to imagine forgiveness as a key to complete the narrative, which also indicated mimetic coherence as a way to find an answer to the narrative. In this instance of explanation, Oliver was an engaged reader.

Lastly, Oliver's seventh reaction is described as an "assessment" where Nawal "succeeded in forgetting the past." He categorized this reaction in Reflection (I), which is an investigation into the affective nature of the text and the effects of the scene (e.g., "I was sad when I read the play because the death of X character provoked my sadness. It's a sad scene"). This reaction points to the axiological judgment category, for the reader validates Nawal's letter by attributing a verb "succeed" that justifies her actions. Furthermore, the text does not provide evidence that Nawal turned the page on her past, thus indicating that Oliver used his fantasmical activity to find answers to the text. These are additional traces of Oliver's reading engagement.

Simon's Accompanying Commentary

I placed my aesthetigram in chronological order, from bottom to top. [Simon describes how each post-it (sticky note) is organized, with its level of importance in the top right corner of each reaction, the category on the top left corner, and a summary of the reaction in the middle of each post-it. We see his will to communicate the structure of completed aesthetigram, without having access to the original post-its]. The arrows represent links between my reactions, each of these [arrows] leads to another [reaction]. One exception to this rule is my reaction on the bottom right corner. This reaction (taste) was not linked to the others. It was just a short-lived moment.

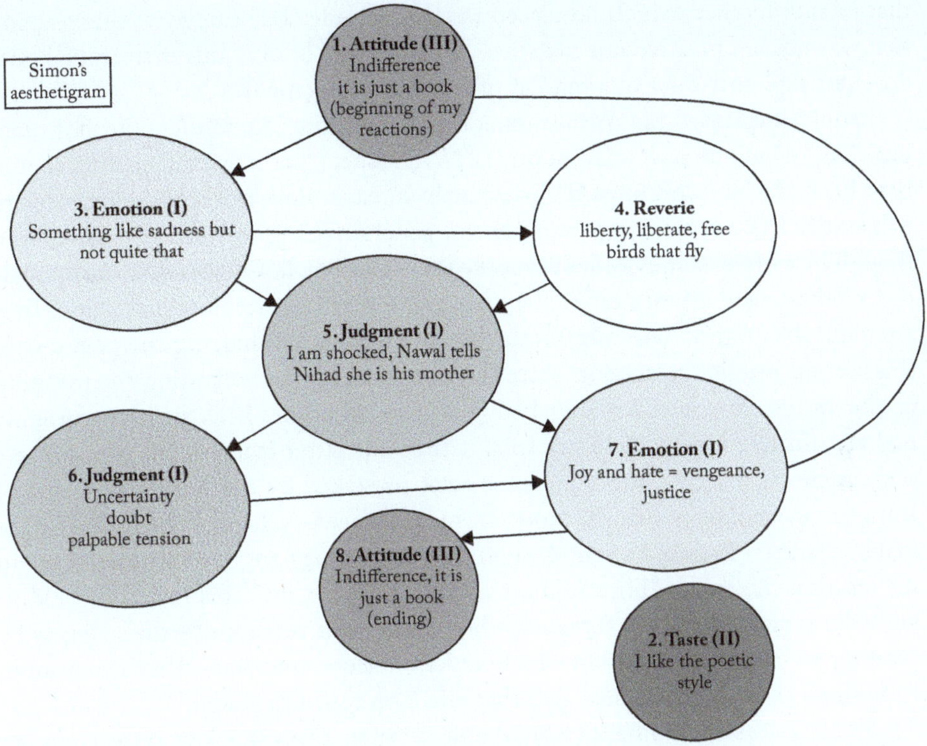

Figure 10: Simon's aesthetigram in response to scene 37 in the play *Incendies*.

I start by being indifferent, I told myself that it was just a book. Then, I enjoyed the poetic style and I started understanding the meaning of the words. This is when I had my first emotion. After that, I started to think about birds, that they are free. Then, I was shocked, Nawal tells her son that she is his mother. Then, I had doubts, I do not know if she was right or wrong in telling him the news. Nevertheless, something in me—like vengeance, justice—is present. But why bother? After all, it is just a book.

Analysis of Simon's Traces of Reading Engagement

Simon included eight reactive moments in his aesthetigram. In his commentary he emphasized his need to draw an organized, tight map. He further detailed how he visually structured his individual moments, as well as the relationships between each moment. He also understood that his reaction "I like the poetic style," placed in the Taste (II) category, was fleeting, which is the reason he separated it from his other reactions. Placed at the top of his aesthetigram, Simon's first reaction was that of indifference, which he placed in the Attitude (III) category; this reaction that was neither positive nor negative: "… it is just a book". This metatextual note does not explicitly refer to a marker of reading engagement.

Simon expressed his third moment as "something like sadness but not quite like that," which he put in Emotion (I). In retrospect, perhaps this reaction should have been placed in Feelings (IVb), whereby a reader does not have a precise word to identify the emotion, and represents a general feeling towards the work, even though he cannot name or identify it precisely. But like in Oliver's case, mapping is not a definite activity whereby categories and limitations are fixed and static. They are malleable. Simon wrote in his justification that after enjoying the poetic style (his second reaction, placed in Taste (II)), he "started understanding the meaning of the words. This is when [he] had [his] first emotion." This reaction certainly had an affective impact. Simon explains that this latter reaction led him to have a moment of "reverie," an imaginative state provoked by the reaction—a sort of Buberian synesthesia with the work. In his commentary, he described that imaginative state as "I started to think about birds, that they are free," and he wrote in his reaction the words "liberty, liberate, free birds that fly." This reaction could fit with the visual realization category, where the reader reacts to textual triggers by creating an imaginary world in which he feels↔sees↔interacts with the narrative. In Simon's case, the birds have had that effect on him as a reader.

In his successive moments, Simon noted: "Then, I was shocked, Nawal tells her son that she is his mother." Simon placed this fifth reaction in the centre of the aesthetigram, and categorized it as Judgment (I). Judgment (I) denotes a spontaneous, initial reaction in which the reader qualifies the character (exaggerated, being clumsy, or other adjectives). In this case, Simon's fifth reaction—shock—is his spontaneous and initial response to Nawal's action. However, he does not qualify the action per se. That is, he does not condemn or approve Nawal's telling of the truth. Therefore, this reaction could not correspond to Langlade's axiological judgment category of reading engagement. Rather, the reaction could have been placed in Explanation II, where the dominating reaction is either one of perplexity or confusion. Shock is a form of perplexity, and doubt (as expressed in reaction 6: "I had doubts, I do not know if she was right or wrong in telling him the news") is a form of confusion. The shock and doubt are indicators of reading engagement if we consider Langlade's definition of the reader's malaise. Placed in Emotion (I), Simon's seventh reaction illustrates the following words: "joy and hate = vengeance. Justice". Simon clarified this equation in his commentary: "Nevertheless, something in me—like vengeance, justice—is present." Vengeance is a powerful emotional and affective response that he identified as his own and surely points to engagement.

Simon concludes his aesthetigram with a statement of indifference (as he puts it), which he placed in Attitude (III). He adds in his justification "But why bother?

After all, it is just a book." Despite the felt indifference Simon depicted at the beginning and end of his aesthetigram, his reverie moments and malaises show that he was at least temporarily engaged.

Simon's emphasis on "it's just a book" points to a larger context that encompasses a general attitude towards reading, or simply a kind of detachment in the moment. It is a contextual state that St. Clair (2005) would call a superunknown. However, causes for attitudes that precede the practice of reading must be the topic of a different study. Here, I confine my research to indicators of engagement. Simon found himself engaged in the story in the moments noticed in this analysis.

Justin's Accompanying Commentary

I separated my aesthetigram into four distinct parts. These parts are related to the central point which is the emotion of sadness. I judged that it was a striking moment in my reading and especially in the *Letter to the Son*. So the first part represents attitude. There are two, because I thought her mood changed as she was writing. The second part of my aesthetigram is the reflections that I had during my reading. There are many of them, so I placed them one next to the other.

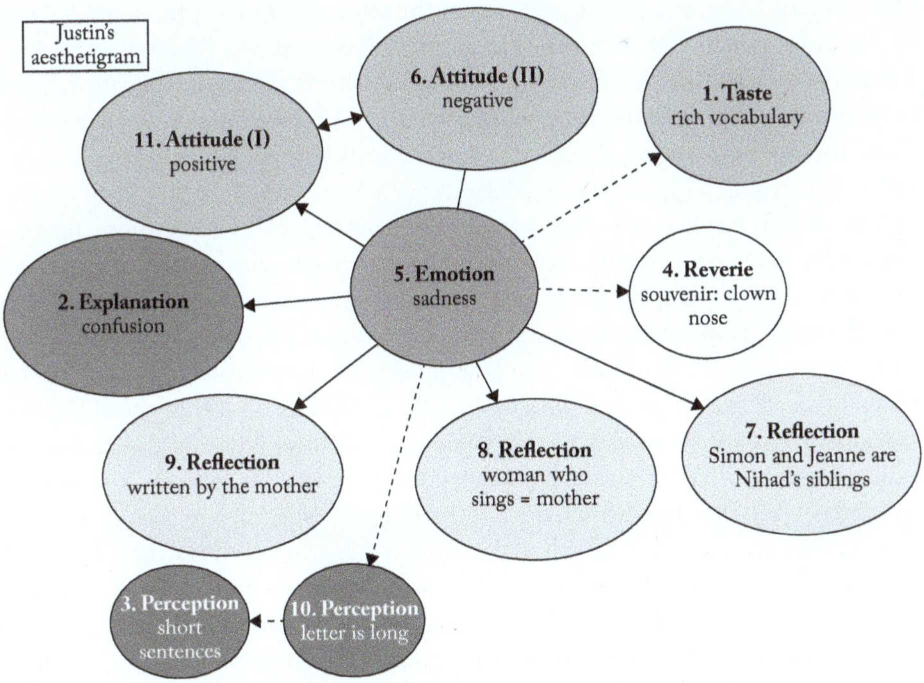

Figure 11: Justin's aesthetigram in response to scene 37 in the play *Incendies*.

Then, my third part has to do with why things happen. Why is she reacting that way? Because, in my opinion, she was confused. Finally, my last part represents the ideas that are not important, I remembered the clown nose, the richness of the vocabulary, that the letter was long and that the sentences were short. All in all, it was the justification of my choices for how I placed my categories and my reactions.

Analysis of Justin's Traces of Reading Engagement

Justin identified eleven moments in his map, which is subdivided into four parts. The reactions are placed within seven categories. The participant did not specify the sub-category for all reactions except the two Attitude ones, placed at the top of his aesthetigram. Justin noted that his central reaction was one of sadness, which he placed in the Emotion category, and described the decision thusly: "I judged that it was a striking moment in my reading and especially in *The Letter to the Son.*" It is difficult to determine the type of reading engagement that this moment suggests, for such analysis would require more detail (e.g., Is the reader referring to his own sadness as he reads, or Nawal's?). However, Justin's affective response is one where he felt one (of many potential) general emotions conveyed by the letter. Justin described his reactions that he put at the top were ones he placed respectively in Attitude (I) and Attitude (II). He wrote: "There are two [reactions], because I thought *her mood changed as she was writing*". Attitude (I) determines the reader's own positive attitude as he reads, while Attitude (II) represents the reader's negative attitude when reading. As described in the aesthetigram guide to reactions, the Attitude categories identify the reader's stance when reading, thus referring to his sadness, which implies empathy as an engagement signifier. Furthermore, Justin is engaged through axiological judgment, for he makes a judgment on Nawal's mood.

Justin's comments regarding his reflections are somewhat limited, and they would benefit from more detail on content. Instead, his focus is on the structure of moments: "… I placed them [the moments] one next to the other." In his map, Justin identified three moments (reactions #7, #8, and #9) in the Reflection category. Moment #7 points to the following sentence: "Simon and Jeanne are Nihad's siblings." Without a sub-category to guide the declaration, it is difficult to understand what Justin means by this sentence, especially in terms of intent. Was Justin surprised that Simon and Jeanne are Nihad's siblings? Or is this just a statement without surprise? The lack of textual triggers like "I think" does not lead to a reflection. If Justin's statement was one of surprise, then having placed this reaction in the Emotion (I) or Explanation (II) categories would have made sense and could have pointed to the reader's malaise (Langlade, 2015) as a form of engagement. Without these indicators, it is difficult to make concrete links with reading engagement.

Reflections #8 and #9 point to a similar, neutral statement "woman who sings = mother" and "written by the mother". These reactions—simply listed here—would benefit from more detail, either in the reactions themselves or in the commentary. For the same reasons as with the previous reaction, it is difficult to suggest links between Justin's reactions and engagement with the text. The participant continues, writing in his commentary: "my third part has to do with why things happen. Why is she reacting that way? Because, in my opinion, she was confused." The latter phrase is linked to reaction #2, where Justin wrote "confusion." He categorized the reaction as Explanation, without specifying the sub-category of his reaction.

The two descriptions provided in the Explanation category relate to either a positive reaction since the reader sees the text as a puzzle, a sign to decode, a problem to solve (Explanation I) or a negative reaction where the dominating feeling is one of puzzlement or confusion, a lack of access to the truth. We can only speculate whether Justin experienced a positive or negative reaction, and it is not my aim. His commentary, however, leads us to think it was the second option: "Why is she reacting that way? Because, in my opinion, she was confused." There are two levels of confusion in that statement: Justin's confusion ("Why is she reacting that way?") and Justin's opinion that Nawal is confused ("Because, in my opinion, she was confused"). The first level could be related to the reader's malaise (Langlade, 2015) in an attempt to complete the narrative (mimetic coherence), while the second statement has more to do with fantasmical activity, since we have no concrete evidence that Nawal is actually confused. The fantasy is more determined in this case by Justin's added interpretation linked to axiological judgment.

Justin concludes his commentary by stating: "Finally, my last part represents the ideas that are not important: clown nose, short sentences, etc." The participant considers moments #4 (Reverie), #1 (Taste), #3 (Perception), and #10 (Perception) to be unimportant. Based on the size of the circles in which the reactions are drawn, these reactions were less meaningful to Justin. Moment #4 describes the recollection of the clown nose, categorized in Reverie (not a memory, but rather an imaginative state provoked by the reaction, a synergy with the work, an immersion in the work that makes the reader forget about time). There is no further indication or detail that helps us determine that his fourth moment is one where he was engaged. That is, how did his remembering the clown nose indicate a synergy with the scene? How does remembering the clown nose provoke an imaginative state? With more detail, we might have had access to clearer indicators of engagement.

Justin's first reaction about the rich vocabulary seemed more important, judging by the size of his circle. The link between his central reaction and his

Taste reaction points to a relationship between form and affect, which suggests engagement (aesthetic impact). However, there is a lack of concrete evidence of engagement, as there is not sufficient commentary that can lead to that conclusion, especially since Justin emphasized that this reaction was not so important to him. Reactions #3 and #10, placed in Perception (a sub-category indicating observations and descriptions towards style) reflect the length of the letter and its short sentences. Overall, despite several reactive moments (13) in Justin's aesthetigram, there is a lack of evidence of reading engagement because of the lack of detail in his commentary. It is apparent, however, that some moments (like his second reaction, and his reflection moments) point to traces of reading engagement.

Noah's Accompanying Commentary

I based my aesthetigram on my most dominant reaction during my reading of the *Letter to the Son*, that is, my astonishment towards the structure of the "poem"

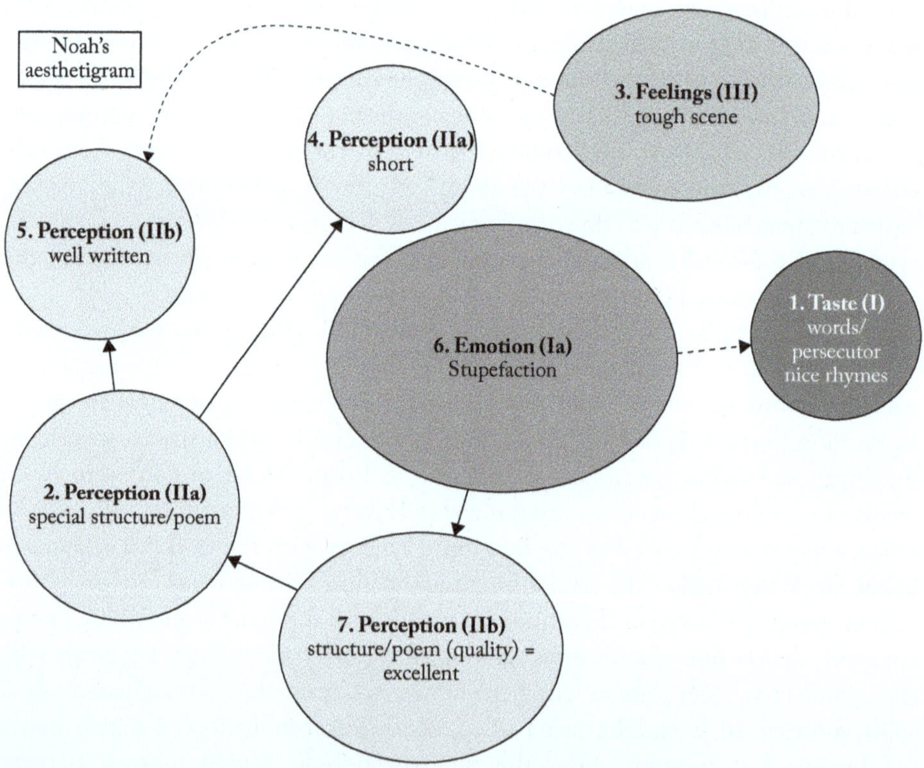

Figure 12: Noah's aesthetigram in response to scene 37 in the play *Incendies*.

that I found excellent. That is why I detailed the structure on my aesthetigram. Then, I thought the scene was really tough and I thought this tension was linked to my feeling of astonishment. That is also why I found that this text was well written. My "weakest" reaction was the rhyme between the words and persecutor that I really liked, but that I found was less relevant. So I put it further away from my other reactions.

Analysis of Noah's Traces of Reading Engagement

Noah's map illustrated seven main moments placed within five categories. His central reaction, described as "astonishment," was placed in category Emotion (Ia), which is a sub-category of feelings. The term "astonishment" would thus point to the term Noah associated with what he felt in that moment. Noah's aesthetigram provides a good example of potential problems in categorizing reactions, because the sub-category "Ia" did not exist in the guide. There are still traces of reading engagement through his accompanying commentary. Noah emphasized that the poem's structure was linked to his affective response. Similarly to Oliver's case, his surprise was linked to the fact that he discovered that the son who brought joy was also the perpetrator of Nawal's sadness.

In Noah's case, the astonishment is linked to the letter's structure. As such, Noah even qualified the letter (a scene from the play) as a poem. Noah's remark and categorization fall within Lacelle and Langlade's (2007) category of "aesthetic impact", for the reader's meaning-making supposes concrete links between affect and form. Noah explained that his central emotion—astonishment—influenced his interest in the text's structure. The latter developed into observations about other perceptions, for example, his awareness of tension in the scene, and his judgment highlighting that the text was well written. These observations appear in his reaction #7 ("structure/poem (quality)=excellent"), reaction #2 ("special structure/ poem"), moment #5 ("well written"), moment #4 ("short"), and reaction #3 ("tough scene"). Noah placed moments #5 and #7 in the Perception (IIb) category, which is a descriptive moment or tendency to identify aspects of the narrative, with a subjective emphasis on preferences about an aspect of the narrative, a subject, theme, or form.

Noah put reactions #2 and #4 in the "Perception (IIa)" category, a description that places selective and specific emphasis on aspects such as form or stylistic devices. These perception moments are, again, linked to the effect of form on affect, that is, aesthetic impact (Lacelle & Langlade, 2007). Noah's third reaction ("tough scene") was placed in Feelings (III)—an affective orientation directed towards a generic expression in which the reader supposes that others will interpret (or should interpret) the work the same way he does. This reaction shows traces of reading engagement through his empathy for the narrative situation. Through his categorization in Feelings (III), Noah showed a desire to interpret this scene as one that triggered emotions in him.

Noah concluded his commentary by indicating that he was interested in the text's rhymes. These sentences could indicate Noah's meaning underlying his first reaction, which he positioned in the Taste (I) category. Even though Noah stated this reaction was less relevant than others, when we look at it holistically with other components of his aesthetigram, it speaks to the other reactions he mapped. That is, Noah's astonishment (affective state) impacts his perception and preferences for form, and these are markers of reading engagement.

Josh's Accompanying Commentary

I put my [emotion] category in the center because I think that it is the sentence that contains all the emotions in the letter. I think that the author should have focused his attention on that [sentence]. Actually, I don't like how the letter was structured. "I searched for you" comes too early in the text. We are still thinking about the letter to the father [the preceding scene] and the contrast is too intense. This leads to an enumeration that is way too long and completely useless

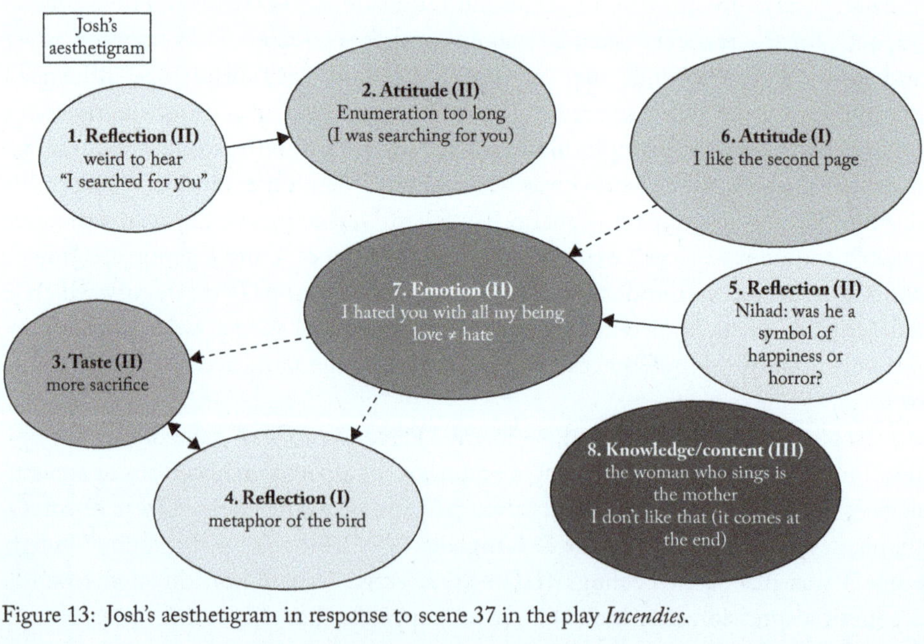

Figure 13: Josh's aesthetigram in response to scene 37 in the play *Incendies*.

[detailing] the places where she searched for him. However, I liked when the text talked about sacrifice. He [the author] should have talked more about that (to express how much she suffered). I also liked the metaphor of the bird. I had no trouble imagining it. What I was not pleased with was when she said: "This letter will tell you that the woman who sings was your mother" (or something like that). Throughout the letter, she remained vague, but incomprehensible, and, suddenly, she says it clearly. (I put this reaction aside because there is no link with my other reactions). In conclusion: rewrite and focus.

Analysis of Josh's Traces of Reading Engagement

Josh placed eight reactive moments in his map, which were distributed among six categories. His central reaction, emotions, was his most important one and he wrote: "'I hated you with all my being' love ≠ hate." Josh placed this reaction in the Emotion (II) category, to acknowledge a combination of terms—attraction *and* repulsion, anger *and* admiration, and so forth. In his reaction, love and hate are juxtaposed. His opinion is a metareflection on the emotions that he perceived were part of the letter ("I think that it is the sentence that contains all the emotions in the letter"). It is possible that Josh's perceived emotions are the ones he felt himself as a reader. That is, there seems to be a distance between thought and emotion in this reaction. Josh's judgment on what the author should have focused on, or have written, is linked to axiological judgment as an engagement indicator. That is, the reader expresses a judgment on content through a critique of the author.

Josh expressed his dislike of the structure of the letter, explaining how, in his opinion, the phrase "I searched for you" came too early. This comment corresponds to reactions #1 and #2 in his aesthetigram. Reaction #1 specifies that he thought it was "weird to hear 'I searched for you'," and its placement within the Reflection (II) category represents a reflection on specific content like a character's specific action (e.g., "I wonder if Nawal knew that her son was the perpetrator"). While Josh categorized his reaction as a reflection (which would have implied a statement like "I wonder"), but it could also have been placed in perception or judgment (e.g., "I find it weird that"). The difference between both affirmations is barely noticeable, but it becomes important in situating manifestations of engagement. The participant's reflection, masked as a judgment "it is weird that," represents an event where, again, he shares his judgment on a sentence. Based only on this reaction in his aesthetigram, I cannot specifically qualify this reaction as one linked to axiological judgment. Doing so would be overanalyzing Josh's statement, where he only finds the sentence to be "weird." However, his accompanying commentary suggests that Josh is, in fact, making a judgment on the text's structure. Three consecutive phrases—"I don't like how/comes too early/the contrast is too intense"—indicate that, in fact, Josh is making an axiological judgment. Josh's values clash with what is written, and he expresses a desire for what "should have been."

His second reaction follows a similar pattern. Josh stated that the enumeration was too lengthy ("way too long and completely useless"). Again, Josh expressed a judgment on the author's writing. He placed this reaction in Attitude (II), which represents his own negative attitude towards the text. He is engaged insofar as this relates to Langlade's axiological judgment. In addition, Josh wrote about his sixth reaction ("the second page"): "I liked when the text talked about sacrifice." Josh placed this comment in the Attitude (I) category, which describes Josh's positive attitude as he reads. Indeed, Josh expressed his likes about the theme, but also his dislikes in his reaction #3. Coherently, Josh placed this latter moment in Taste (II) category. Both reactions illustrate Josh's opinion towards what is "right" about the text and what he imagined should have been written.

Josh continued to be engaged as he exercised his axiological judgment. As such, he provided substantial detail through his agreement and rejection moments regarding the style and themes of the written scene. In other words, it was not just a fleeting moment of opinion towards *what might have been* present in the scene. His opinions are manifested through different moments towards different aspects of the scene. Josh wrote about his fourth moment that he "liked the metaphor of the bird," and that he "had no trouble imagining it." He placed this reaction in Reflection (I), which is an investigation into the affective nature of the text (i.e., what the scene provokes in the reader). While Josh did not provide further detail regarding "what the scene provoked" in him, he did comment about imagination and how easy it was for him to picture this metaphor. There is a moment of engagement as this reaction shows a trace of visual realization. Josh described his moment #8 in his map as "the woman who sings is the mother. I don't like that [it comes at the end]," and added in his commentary that he felt displeasure with the letter's ending, for the truth was not clearly communicated at first.

Josh classified this reaction in Knowledge/Content (III) (i.e., when the reader uses an intellectual lens to understand the content, with an emphasis on 'other considerations'). Knowledge/Content (III) compares to a form of detachment from the text, with further considerations not present in the guide to reactions that allow for an expansion of the reader's own ideas. Josh's commentary confirms that his reaction was about his own judgment towards the text and indeed "what should have been." His objections are about the sequence of the letter this time, and his explanations are lengthier. Thus, Josh was engaged in this reaction through his axiological judgment. In his fifth reaction, Josh observed "Nihad: was he a symbol of happiness or horror?" which he placed in the Reflection (II) category, representing a reflection on specific content like a character's action (e.g., "I wonder if Nawal knew that her son was the perpetrator"). In this moment, Josh reflected on the main themes of the scene, with a specific emphasis on Nihad. Josh did not judge, but rather reflected on this instance. As such, his reaction can be associated with mimetic coherence, as he attempted to clarify this element of the plot through his reflection. Josh concluded his accompanying commentary with: "In conclusion: rewrite and focus." This final statement suggests a holistic view of his *gestalt*, that is, the sum of his moments that indicate his engagement through his axiological judgment, visual realization, and mimetic coherence. Through his recommendations to the author, Josh expressed judgments that were mostly negative, yet he still proved to be an engaged reader.

Max's Accompanying Commentary

I placed the reaction of hate in the center of my aesthetigram because I think that the most important thing in the *Letter to the Son* was the mother's reaction. She hates her son because he raped her, but she forgives him because he is her son. I put

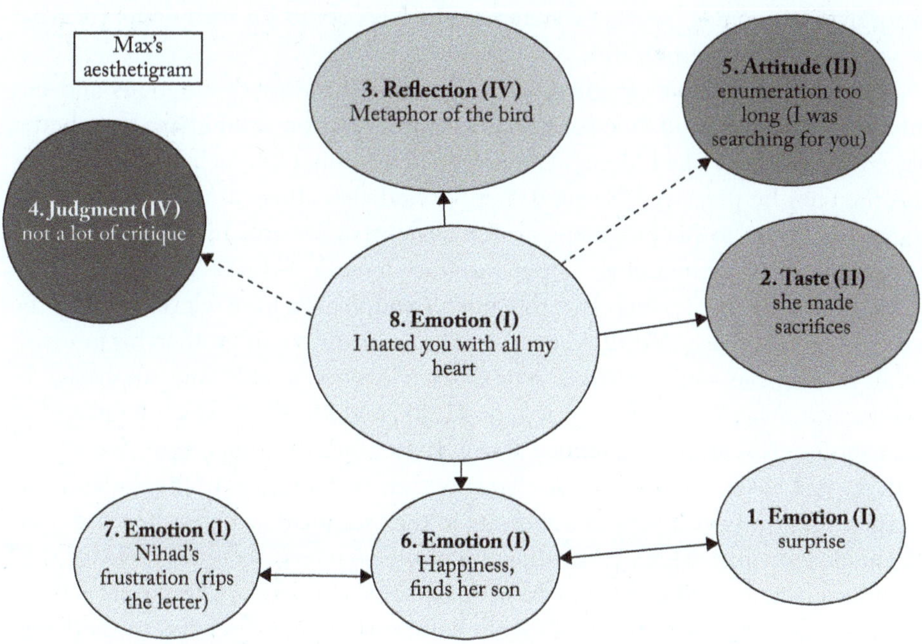

Figure 14: Max's aesthetigram in response to scene 37 in the play *Incendies*.

the three "emotion" reactions at the bottom because these are the feelings that the mother and the son have felt throughout the letter. The frustration of Nihad, who learns all that he did to his mother. His mother's joy in finding her son and the surprise when Nihad learns this. However, I thought that the repetition of "I searched for you" was a bit too long, it resurfaces too often on the same page. I liked the fact that the mother explained that she made tons of sacrifices in order to find her son. This shows the very strong bond between a mother and her son. Unfortunately, when I read the letter again, I did not feel a lot of things.

Analysis of Max's Traces of Reading Engagement

Max noted eight reactions in his aesthetigram, divided into five main categories. Max placed his central reaction in the Emotion (I) category and justified it with this in-text quotation: "I hated you with all my heart." As such, Max made a judgment on Nawal's action (she hates her son but ultimately forgives him), and this judgment is part of Langlade's assigning axiological judgment as a trace of reading engagement. It is also an attempt to complete the narrative (mimetic coherence) based on Max's fantasmic activity (desire to see the narrative from his own perspective). That is, the text does not provide us with the fact that Nawal hates and/or forgives her son. It is rather a statement by Max about his own desire for what he wants to see in the narrative.

Since the Emotion category has to do with the reader's emotions and not the characters' projected emotions, Max's central reaction would have been better placed in a category like Judgment. There is a detachment between Max's emotions and the ones he perceived Nawal to feel. Nonetheless, there are traces of reading engagement due to his judgment on the character's actions. In his commentary, Max continues by explaining: "I put the three 'emotion' reactions at the bottom because these are the feelings that the mother and the son have felt throughout the letter. *The frustration of Nihad*, who learns all that he did to his mother; his mother's joy in finding her son and *the surprise when Nihad learns this*" (my emphasis). In this excerpt, Max refers to his reactions #1, #7, and #6, all of which he placed in the Emotion (I) category described above. These three reactions, again, have to do with the perceived emotions of the characters rather than those of the reader. These moments might have been more accurate in the Judgment category. Because these reactions described Max's perceptions of the characters, they disclose traces of reading engagement that have to do with axiological judgment, fantasmic activity, and mimetic coherence. That is, Nihad's emotions are not disclosed in the letter; Max attempted to complete the narrative through his own imaginative states using his perception of what happened.

Max recorded one moment (#5) in Attitude (II), which represents his own negative attitude about repetition of the phrase 'I searched for you.' It is interesting to note that this statement of fact was impactful for three students, and each of them interpreted it differently. Josh thought it was weird and that it came too early, and Max thought it was too long. Since these are comments regarding the author's style, they have to do with axiological judgment as traces of reading engagement.

Max put his second reaction in the Taste (II) category, which points to a preference for an aspect of the narrative (e.g., "I like the description of the bird in the text"). His commentary refers to further moments of taste: "I *liked* the fact that ...." Max follows this statement with a judgment: "This *shows* the very strong bond between a mother and her son" (my emphasis). These moments of taste and judgment are examples of Max's engagement.

Max placed moment #3 in Reflection (IV), a category that has to do with the text's aesthetics. Max did not provide further detail regarding this moment, and simply wrote "metaphor of the bird" in his reaction. Max situated his fourth moment in Judgment (IV), which depicts a deliberate abstention of judgment. His reaction might have been linked to his last sentence in the commentary: "Unfortunately, when I read the letter again, I did not feel a lot of things." This last comment

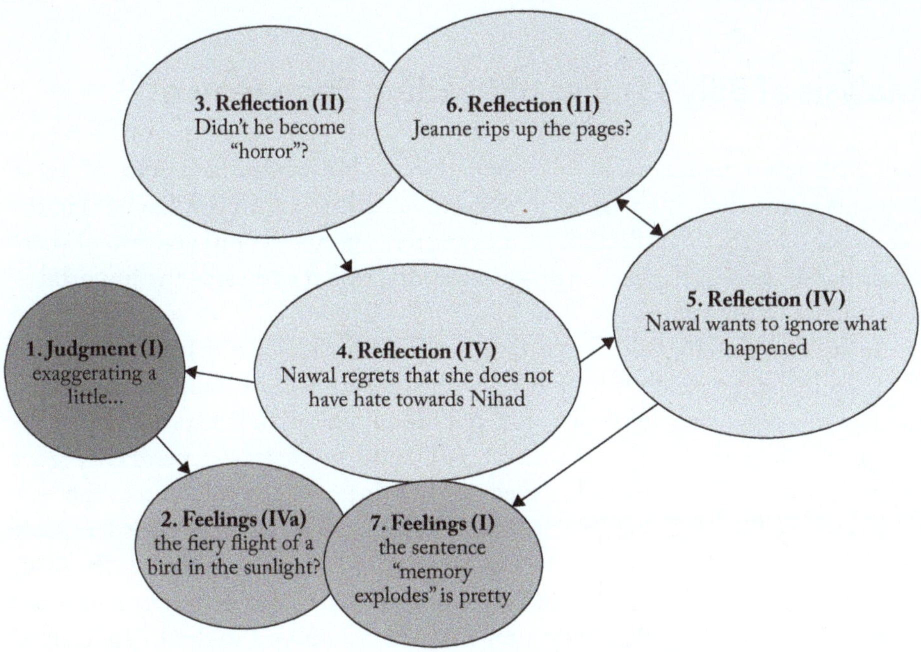

Figure 15: Billy's aesthetigram in response to scene 37 in the play *Incendies*.

speaks to the rest of his aesthetigram, for it portrays an example of the participant's abilities to distance himself from the narrative and helps him analyze it. His engagement is more analytical than emotional.

Billy's accompanying commentary:

I chose to put reaction #4 in the center [of the aesthetigram] because I think it explains well the atmosphere or the way that Nawal narrates the letter. She says she loves her son, but we feel that she really feels hate towards him. It is why reaction #5 is linked to the center, because it also reflects well Nawal's thinking and her reaction, that is to ignore what happened. Reaction #5 is linked to reaction #6 because Jeanne rips up the pages maybe to forget what happened, but I am not sure. Reaction #3 is linked to the center because Nawal says that Nihad went from being horror to happiness (sic) but I think that it is contrary to what happened. Reaction #1 is linked to the center because I think that Nihad exaggerates in the letter. That is why reaction #2 is linked to reaction #1, because I do not really understand what she means by "the fiery flight of a bird in the sunlight," because she used words that exaggerated the meaning. I linked reaction #2 and #7 because they represent reactions of taste regarding word choice. Finally, reaction #3 and #6 are linked because they are questions.

Analysis of Billy's Traces of Reading Engagement

Billy had seven moments in his aesthetigram. He categorized four of these moments in the Reflection category, with two of them (reactions #3 and #6) in the second sub-category (a reflection on a character's specific action) and two of them (reaction #4 and #5) in the fourth sub-category, which addresses the importance of aesthetics of the text.

In his reaction #6, Billy noted that he "was not sure" about Jeanne's motives to rip up the letter which is indicative of the reader's will to complete the narrative as a way of making sense out of it. The "doubt phase" Billy expressed matches Langlade's category of mimetic coherence. Doubt specifies the type of coherence the student makes as he reads. In other words, this term adds precision to the type of investment Billy is going through, and shares similarities with what Langlade (2015) later called the reader's "interrogations" (p. 51), or questionnings. The association between a reflective state and the will to understand is definitely important for Billy. Response #3 is definitely a reflection that implies a desire to understand (mimetic coherence): "*I think that* [the move from horror to happiness] *it is contrary to what happened*" (my emphasis). In other words, Billy disagrees with the explanation in the text. He argues that Nihad was a source of joy because Nawal looked for her son first (happiness), and then discovered that she was one of his victims (horror). This latter statement further translates into fantasmic activity, for Billy builds on his desires to plan and express what he thinks is the truth.

Billy's responses #4 and #5 were categorized in Reflection (IV), a theme that has to do with the text's aesthetics. Billy noted that his fourth reaction "explains well the atmosphere or *the way in which* Nawal narrates the letter. She says she loves her son, *but we feel that she really feels* hate towards him" (my emphasis). Billy's comment points to another occasion where he disagrees with what is written in the text—regardless of the "truth," his observations are indicative of a reflective involvement. Looking at Langlade's typology, this response could be classified in the mimetic coherence, visual realization, and aesthetic impact categories. That is, by placing his response in the Reflection (IV) category, Billy was likely aware that the aesthetics of the text had an impact on his thinking and reflection, leading him to comment on how the text augments the love/hate duality he imagined when reading the letter. In addition, the *Letter to the Son* is quite metaphorical (e.g., repetitions of "I searched for you," numerous alliterations, metaphors, and figures of speech implying aesthetic impact), and the reactions Billy had certainly aimed to complete the text (mimetic coherence).

Furthermore, Billy's comments on the imagined way in which Nawal narrated the letter most likely triggered his visual realization, for there is no detail in the text that describes the atmosphere. These intricacies were only present in the reader's mind (visual realization). In addition, Billy's fourth response shows traces of empathy: "but we feel that she really feels," shows an example of the reader's engagement through his fictional empathy (Brett, 2016; Larrivé, 2015). Billy's fifth response revealed a judgment: "Nawal wants to ignore what happened." Here, Billy interpreted the meaning of Nawal's letter to fit his understanding of the story. That is, in his will to complete the text (mimetic coherence), Billy built on his own interpretation even though there is no clear indication that it coincides with Nawal's thinking (fantasmic activity). One could place this Reflection response in the mimetic coherence and fantasmic activity categories. The reader's "delirium" (Langlade, 2006) transposes his own reading engagement as he fictionalizes his desires while reading.

Billy noted that his first response was one he placed in Judgment (I), which is "a spontaneous, initial reaction whereby he judged character Z to be exaggerating/happy/clumsy/etc.". Billy explained that one of the characters was exaggerating in the letter. The judgment category naturally relates back to Langlade's axiological judgment, as Billy expressed his judgment on the character's action. It is difficult to know if Billy is referring to Nihad's exaggeration, as Nihad is not the one who wrote the letter. It poses the question: "Why would Nihad exaggerate if he did not write the letter?" This response is a form of fantasmic activity; if Billy is really talking about Nihad exaggerating, he is inventing events that are not explicitly taking place in the letter. Rather than seeing this commentary as negative (e.g., he did not understand), fantasmic activity as a form of engagement posits that Billy's impulses to imagine what did not (or has not yet) happen is a positive form of reading engagement.

Finally, responses #2 and #7 were placed in the Feelings category. Billy placed response #2 in Feelings (IVa)—an emotionally oriented category, with a series of words that describe a subjective meaningful emotion towards a subject, a sentence, or a structure in particular. Billy judged that the words were exaggerated, and he seemed puzzled by this: "I do not really understand what she means by 'the fiery flight of a bird in the sunlight,' because she used words that exaggerated the meaning." Billy's puzzlement, too, is a form of reading engagement, insofar as it raises his interactions with the narrative based on axiological judgment and his own "malaise" as a reader. I evaluate Billy's response considering Rosenblatt's (1978) original framing of the nature of engaged readers, as well as Langlade's (2015) conception of the reader's "malaise" as "destabilisation" (p. 51). In agreement with the evolution of the model describing the moments of engagement through the reader's fictional activity (Lacelle & Langlade, 2007; Langlade, 2004, 2006, 2013, 2015; Langlade & Fourtanier, 2007), the aesthetigram enables the reader to reify his own doubts (or *malaises*). That is, Billy's puzzlement can enrich his reading engagement (Langlade, 2015). The comment on the relationships between affect and form, or what Lacelle and Langlade (2007) would categorize as "aesthetic impact," is multi-layered and complex.

As Billy's aesthetigram illustrates, at times the words read by Billy led to reflections that have to do with doubt, or how feelings can emerge from a consideration of form, or even his understanding of his judgments. Billy's categorizations refined the type of meaning-making that he constructed. For example, response #7 placed in Feelings (I), an emotionally oriented category denoted with words that describe an emotion based on response to sensory elements in the reading. Billy understood that his feelings affected his reading in terms of word choice. This moment comes as a manifestation of aesthetic impact on the reader's reaction.

Portfolio Analysis

In this in-depth analysis, I report the results from Billy's portfolio. This section is more extensive than my review of the other participants of this study. Billy's completed exercises provide a comprehensive review of the additional research tools I used to look at traces of reading engagement.

In his pre-test, Billy detailed what reading engagement meant for him:

> [Being engaged in reading means] being interested by the book, either by the characters and their storyline, or by the plot in general. Being engaged in reading happens when you finish reading a paragraph of a page, and you want to continue reading to know more right away. It's a bit like being engaged in watching a TV show; you just can't stop watching it.

According to his definition, Billy put emphasis on multiple facets of engagement: the idea of being curious, or interested by, the book's characters, their story, and the intrigue. Looking at the reviews of reading engagement, a marked interest for the characters is subject to empathy-making and judgment-making. That is, the mental processes one undergoes as he reads presupposes such actions. Furthermore, Billy's emphasis on the reading pace and rhythm, as well as the motivation to continue reading, speak to Bertrand Gervais' (2006) distinction and balance between reading-as-progression and reading for comprehension. That is, there is an equilibrium between reading rapidly/superficially, and reading very slowly with considerable interest. This act should be fast (or slow) enough to allow the student to read through a flow (Csikszentmihalyi, 1990) that reflects the reader's engagement. Billy's comparison with being hooked by a TV series is a valid illustration, or mental image, of what reading engagement could represent for him.

In the multiple-choice question that aims to assess students' understanding of the concept of reading engagement, Billy checked the following answers:

Being engaged in reading means:

1. Being moved by the plot and characters;
2. Becoming attached to characters;
3. Imagining the rest of the story;
4. Judging characters' actions;
5. Feeling empathy for characters.

Billy's answers to this multiple-choice question speak to the detailed response he gave for the first question on reading engagement. Selecting answers #2, #4, and #5, echo reading engagement as a way of "being interested in the story, the characters and their storyline," and reiterates the need for empathy and judgment towards the characters as a feature of reading engagement. Answer #1 mirrors Gervais' concept of reading-as-progression, whereas response #3 reveals an understanding of reading engagement that mirrors Langlade's mimetic coherence, whereby the reader completes the narrative to fill the gaps (taking into consideration Eco's model reader).

In the first part of the reading questionnaire, which addresses axiological judgment, Billy wrote that the following excerpt made him hate Simon:

> *The excerpt that* ***shocked*** *me and that made me hate a character was at the beginning when Simon is mad at his mom and he insults her and says he will spit on her corpse. I understand that he is mad about the testament, but I mean* ***he really goes too far***. *She's* ***still his mother.***

Billy's response shows diverse layered traces of reading engagement. His first response, that of being "shocked," reminds us of Langlade's (2015) concept of the reader's malaise. Furthermore, he seems to have a genuine concern for the characters, for both Nawal and Simon, outlining traces of reading engagement through empathy. He shows an empathetic understanding for Simon, insofar as he understands why the character would feel anger towards his mother. However, Billy asserts that anger should be constrained by limits: "… *he really goes too far.*" His judgment towards Simon's actions shows an alignment with Billy's own moral values (which can also be considered a form of engagement (cf. White, 2007, 2014)).

Billy wrote further judgments on another character, the notary:

> *At the beginning, I thought the notary Hermile Lebel was annoying because he kept babbling the whole time, but in the end he earned my respect because he helped the twins in many situations to find Nihad. This proves that he can be trusted and that he is wittier than one would think.*

Billy's commentary presents additional traces of reading engagement through axiological judgment. His articulation on the notion of respect, as well as the understanding that helping means trust, shows another tangent towards judgment and moral values (Langlade, 2006; White, 2007, 2014). Looking across Billy's answers, he formulated his axiological judgment towards a wide array of characters, which demonstrates a deeper level of reading engagement with the narrative.

Billy conveyed his hypothetical narrative development as he imagined how he would have acted if he had been in Nawal's shoes:

> *Had I been in Nawal's shoes when she was travelling with Sawda, I would not have killed the military chief.* ***I don't think that it was worth*** *it, because she created even more conflict and as a result she was imprisoned, which ended her quest to find her son (even if she unknowingly met him in prison, it* ***would have been wiser*** *not getting jailed).*

This passage presents two main features of reading engagement: (1) axiological judgment and (2) empathy. Billy expresses his axiological judgment by judging Nawal's decision to kill the chief of the militia, and then condemns her action by advocating against murder and violence. He demonstrates a rationalized comprehension of the consequences of murder, showing a holistic understanding of moral and societal values, which are basic conditions for empathy (Hoffman, 2014). Nussbaum (1998) would categorize Billy's response as one where he is engaged.

Billy continued to talk about his approval of Sawda's actions, strengthening his axiological judgment towards characters of the play. For instance, in his commentary on notary Lebel, Billy brings up the notion of help, and links it this time to the idea of friendship. Moral values are thus embedded in his phrasing through his formulation of the concept of good friendship. As an additional trace of reading engagement, Billy added that he felt empathy for Sawda, based on her will to abandon and sacrifice her own aspirations and desires to prioritize Nawal's:

> *I most became attached to Sawda because I liked her explanation as to why she wanted to leave her hometown and accompany Nawal. She had no one to love and* ***I felt empathy*** *for her. She wants to give* it all to help out *Nawal, which proves that she is a good friend.*

In the second part of the reading questionnaire, I asked questions related to Langlade's visual realization as a feature of reading engagement. I did not expect all students to engage in making drawings, though most did. Billy's drawings speak to that type of engagement, accompanied by his written justifications.

Below his drawing of an alternative book cover he would have preferred to the one that was used, Billy wrote: "In this image, we see Jeanne and Simon who open their mom's letter [testament] and it is burning like the title of the play [*Incendies*]." Billy's meaning-making happens here through his drawing thus revealing hidden literacies (Kendrick & Rowsell, 2014; Rowsell & Kendrick, 2013), which are based on the kinesthetic articulation of the mental images he mobilized when thinking holistically about the play. The culminating point for him is the scene we studied in class.

Billy's illustration speaks to Rowsell and Kendrick's (2013) statement urging researchers to consider drawings as a valid way to uncover the "hidden dimensions of literacy" that boys can produce in order for them to "construct" and "critique" what they read (p. 597). The researchers have found that reluctant boy readers engaged considerably with the act of drawing as a meaning-making practice, and advocate for the complementarity of drawings for engagement in understanding narratives: "the visual promotes student agency by making visible hidden and purloined literacies. Using linguistic modes alone, we would not have acquired a window onto each boy's worlds" (p. 597). Billy's drawings (see more

Figure 16: Billy's drawing of the book cover.

of them in the next section) speak to an additional type of engagement with the narrative, and prove to be a legitimate research tool, focusing on "words *plus* visuals" (Kendrick & Rowsell, 2014, p. 321), through the activities I used in this research project.

In another question that stimulated an articulation of mental images (Brehm, 2008, 2011, 2015), Billy explained the way in which he visualized (Kendrick & Rowsell, 2014; Rowsell & Kendrick, 2013) scene 37:

> *The scene takes place in a room,* ***like it is written*** *in the ending of the preceding scene. Nihad, Jeanne, and Simon are the only ones present in the room. Nihad opens the letter and keeps it in his hands. He reads the letter, but we do not know whether the twins read it too, we only know that Jeanne rips up her note pad at the end of the scene, which means that the search for her brother has ended.*

Billy's description of the imagined setting of scene 37 gives evidence of traces of reading engagement. Billy indeed mobilizes two features of reading engagement, taking into consideration Langlade's model, which are visual realization, mimetic coherence, and fantasmic activity. That is, Billy personalized his imagined sequence of events in scene 37, describing the setting, characters present, and actions (visual realization). He further completes the narrative (mimetic coherence) by offering supplemental details on his perceived interpretation of the scene's ending. Jeanne's action leads to the end of Nawal's quest, as Billy imagines it. This last wording relates back to Langlade's fictional activity. That is, nothing in the letter points to such an interpretation. However, Billy's subjective interpretation speaks to his own engagement as a reader. An invested reader, Billy "intervenes with" the text, and "singularizes" through a one-on-one meeting, his interpretation of the text (Gervais, 1998).

I asked students to further document and explain their own imagined configuration of two characters of their choice. I then asked them to draw their representation of the characters. I designed this activity in line with Kendrick and Rowsell's (2014) conclusion from a study on boys' hidden literacies: "Monomodal writing practices may also lack the action-oriented possibilities of the visual, in both production and form, integral to the meaning-making practices of many boys," (p. 343) but also outlining the complementarity of drawings to response-based literacy practices.

Figure 17: First character: Billy's representation of Nawal in the written play.

Billy's Commentary

> *In the preceding scene, it is written that she is 65 and that she is in the hospital. She narrates the letter, but Nihad does not hear her, he is just reading her letter. By talking to him, she risks forgetting what he has done to her, so she speaks to him like he is her son and not the torturer. She still looks angry and tells him how she felt when she was in her cell. She looks at peace with herself. She still speaks to her twins even though they can't hear her.*

Billy's commentary points to a detailed understanding of Nawal's actions through his visualized interpretations of scene 37. Billy builds on scene 36 as an entry point to the setting in scene 37; contextualizing Nawal's age and action of reading the letter. His dialogic understanding of the interactions of the scenes show a holistic comprehension of, and involvement with, the narrative. Billy's reading engagement is manifested in his writing through visual realization, fantasmic activity, and mimetic coherence. His comments on Nawal's demeanor, perceived anger and serenity are examples of his visual realization. Billy manifests his mimetic coherence and fantasmic activity through the following inference: "by talking to him, she risks forgetting what he has done to her, so she speaks to him like he is her son and not the torturer," meaning that, with Nawal adopting a certain tone, the reader fills certain gaps of the narrative through his imagined stance on what happened.

Figure 18: Second character: Billy's representation of Nihad in the written play.

Nihad was the second character drawn and detailed in Billy's commentary:

> *We don't know Nihad's exact age, but he is an adult. He seems to have been educated and trained by the militia before becoming a marksman, and then he became a sniper. He likes to listen to music and has certain talents in photography. He is pitiless, he kills everybody as he wishes. He stays passive and he does not talk much and he speaks to himself.*

The drawing that accompanies Billy's depiction of Nihad points to different traces of his engagement. As such, Billy mobilizes his mimetic coherence and fantasmic activity, filling gaps from the narrative and rationalizing Nihad's journey through his military education. Billy visually and semantically represented this military training by a gun, indicative of violence. His additional comment on Nihad's merciless personality shows an engagement through visual realization and fantasmic activity, that is, Billy's perception of Nihad's character traits through mental images.

In another question, I asked Billy to describe a particular action Nawal made in scene 37. He answered:

> *She tells Nihad that he has his own kids in front of him, Jeanne and Simon, which is true, but she made sure that the letter would be opened with the twins present. She asked Jeanne to give the letter to her son, but she did not know that they would read the letter together.*

This passage is another example of the articulation of his mimetic coherence and fantasmic activity. That is, Billy makes connections between events of the narrative in order to make sense of it. Scene 37 does not reveal all this information about Nawal's intentions. The reader can only grasp the implications. I then asked Billy to describe his imagined perception of Nawal's voice, demeanor, and attitude as he perceived the character in this particular moment of the play:

> *I imagine that Nawal's voice is calm, but not without emotions. I imagine her as someone who is reciting a poem. I imagine that it is as if she is moving around him in circles in a very calm way and points to Jeanne and Simon when she names them. She almost moves like a ghost. She seems passionate as she wants to convey her emotions to Nihad, her love and her hate.*

Billy's remarks suggest daydream-like (re)configurations of Nawal's tone and posture as she reads the letter. Billy's depictions of Nawal's embodied performance speak to his visual realization of the scene. Finally, Billy was able to further mobilize his visual realization in his response to the question: "What do you think scene 37 will look like in the film?"

> *In the movie, I imagine the scene to be a bit like in the play, that is Nihad reads the letter, but this time Nawal narrates the letter aloud. Nawal speaks to Nihad on a different tone, he does not hear or look at her, but she acts as if he could see her (she points at the twins when she talks about them).*

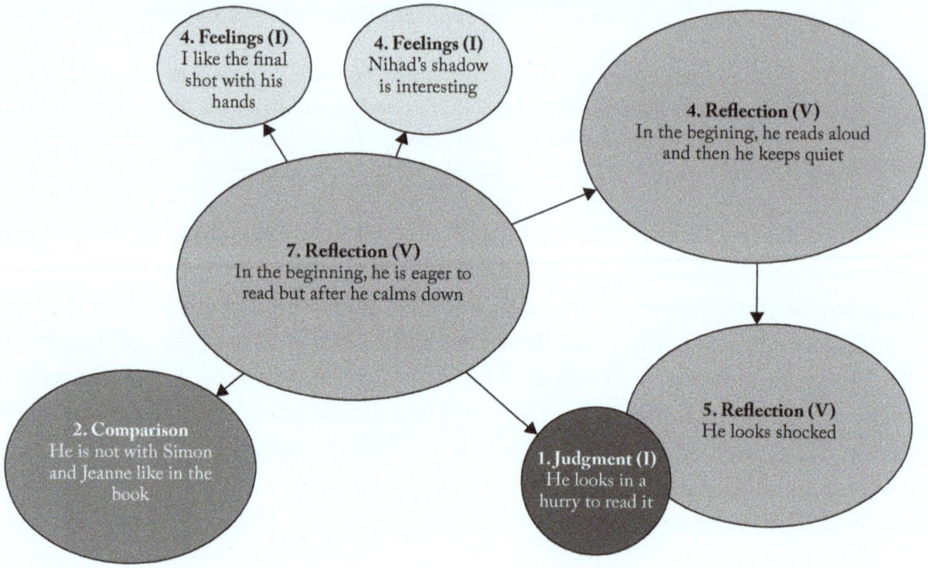

Figure 19: Billy's aesthetigram in response to scene 37 in the film *Incendies*.

Billy's Accompanying Commentary for the Second Aesthetigram

I put reaction 7 in the center because I think it is Nihad's principal reaction when he reads the letter, which is that of discovering the striking conclusion. I put reactions 3 and 6 together, because these are my preferences on the way the scene was shot. Reaction 4 resembles reaction 2, so it has the same level of importance. Responses 1 and 5 are Nihad's feelings so that's why they are placed together and linked to reactions 7 and 4, because they [#1 and #5] are sub-responses [of #7 and #4]. Reaction 2 is a bit set aside because it is a comparison between the film and the written play, it is not really linked to my other reactions.

Analysis of Billy's Traces of Engagement with the Scene of the Film

In his second aesthetigram, Billy noted seven responses to the film's scene 37, which is the same number of responses he wrote for his first aesthetigram. His most impactful response, Billy highlights, was placed in the middle of his aesthetigram in the Reflection (V) category, indicating a prolonged questioning about an overall meaning, and points to the following comment: "I think it is Nihad's principal reaction when he reads the letter, which is that of discovering the striking conclusion." The reaction he wrote in this aesthetigram was directed towards Nihad's reading pace: "in the beginning, he is eager to read but after he calms down." Billy's understanding of Nihad's action speaks to his axiological judgment as a trace of engagement, that is, judging the character on his actions and explaining how the shocking news influences the character's reading pace. This is another trace of visual realization and aesthetic impact, for Billy's imagined mental images frame his understanding of the viewed scene. Billy's fourth response is very similar to his central one. Indeed, he notes: "In the beginning, he reads aloud and then he keeps quiet." Also categorized in Reflection (V), the fourth response points again to Nihad's tone as he reads the letter; the influence of the perceived form on affect, hereby showing traces of engagement through visual realization and aesthetic impact.

Billy further demonstrated a strong organizational concern in his second aesthetigram, as he noted in his accompanying commentary: "Responses 1 and 5 are Nihad's feelings so that's why they are placed together and linked to reactions 7 and 4, because they [#1 and #5] are sub-responses [of #7 and #4]." This note on the aesthetigram's structure illustrates Billy's holistic understanding of the aesthetigram-making procedure, and his need to communicate his meaning-making effectively. Indeed, Billy's fifth response makes the following statement: "he looks shocked," which is a trace of engagement through axiological judgment regarding Nihad's reactions, as well as empathy for Nihad. In other words, Billy's perception is characterized by the ability to feel what Nihad feels, all the while qualifying Nihad's experience as Billy feels it. Concurrently, Billy's first response is described by "he looks in a hurry to read it [the letter]," which is another form of perceived judgment on the action, thus implying axiological judgment. Placed in Judgment (I), Billy's first response is indeed placed in a category that has to do with a spontaneous reaction where the participant spontaneously judges a character's actions.

Billy's responses #3 and #6 were categorized in Feelings (I). That is, an emotionally oriented category with formal elements that describe an emotion based on a response to sensory-oriented elements. Response #3 describes the fact that "Nihad's shadow is interesting," while response #6 establishes that Billy "likes the final shot with [Nihad's] hands." These two observations echo Lacelle and Langlade's (2007) concern with aesthetic impact, for form impacts the viewer's affect: "I have put reactions 3 and 6 together, because these are my preferences on the way the scene was shot."

Billy's second response is a comparison between the elements present in the scene of the film and the play, specifying how the twins are not present in the film's scene 37 as they are in the play. Logically, the participant placed this reaction in the Comparison category, which addresses these concerns. Comparisons provoke another type of engagement, for the participant allows himself to critically detach himself from the two narratives and make associations and distinctions between them. It would be valuable to have further research that addresses comparisons between the written work and the film.

Billy's Ekphrastic Compositions

The following ekphrasis shows Billy's response-as-perceived building from his first aesthetigram in response to scene 37 in the play. As White (2013) found in his research on ekphrastic poetry, ekphrasis allows participants to share empathetic moments through poetic investigations. Billy's writings confirm this finding as a trace of engagement.

Billy wrote:

> *Dear Nihad, I am sorry that I cannot hate you. I would despise you for what you have done if you were not my son, the son I was looking for, for so long. I would love to forget what happened, but it is impossible. When you showed me that little clown nose and my memory exploded, I knew that I could not forget you. You were happiness and you became horror, to then become happiness tinted with horror. When Jeanne rips up this letter, please do not forget me.*
>
> *From Nawal, your mother*

Billy offered the following justification accompanying his letter:

> *I chose the genre of the open letter because I wanted to continue the letter to the son that Nawal wrote including the possible feelings she would have felt for Nihad, even though she has not expressed them in her letter. The best way to continue a letter is obviously to write one.*

Billy's engagement with the scene manifests itself through mimetic coherence, fantasmic activity, and empathy. First, it presupposes empathy with Nawal's situation because Billy made the conscious choice to write a letter in Nawal's name. This technique reminds us of Martin Buber's *I-thou* dialectic, which presupposes a form of embodied response (Sumara, 2002; Sumara, Luce-Kapler & Iftody, 2008), allowing the writer to form a sort of synergy with the object or character in the narrative, thereby provoking empathetic states. Furthermore, Billy explains in his commentary that he chose to write a letter because he wanted to pursue Nawal's "possible feelings she would have felt for Nihad." Only Billy can imagine these feelings through his own fantasmic activity, which is likely triggered by his desire to complete the narrative (Lewkowich, 2015, 2016a, 2016b) through mimetic coherence (Langlade, 2006). Billy comments on the letter writing as a genre that allows for that type of empathetic rendering: "The best way to continue a letter is obviously to write one." It would have been insightful and educational to pursue this lesson explaining how creative writing can lead readers and viewers to produce likely empathetic effects.

Billy created a second ekphrastic piece, this time in response to scene 37 in the movie. He wrote:

> *Dear Nawal,*
>
> *I am writing you this letter with shaky hands. Your kids just left after giving me your letter. I said "your kids," because I could not accept that they were mine. It is true that I was eager to read your letter, but now, I wish I had not read it. When I clicked in the middle of reading the letter, I could not believe it. How could I have hurt my own mother, the one I searched for all this time? I realize how much I have hurt you and it breaks my heart. I know that apologies mean nothing, but I wanted to let you know that I am profoundly affected and regret all that I have done.*
>
> *Your son, Nihad*

Billy offered further insights about his production in his accompanying commentary:

> *I wrote this open letter, because I wanted to demonstrate my understanding of Nihad's reaction when he read the letter. The film and the book do not explain that, so I thought it would be interesting to know what Nihad thinks through a letter to his mother (maybe he does not know that she is dead).*

In symmetry, Billy invented a letter extrapolating Nihad's perceived response to his mother's participant-generated letter. In other words, the second letter, just like the second aesthetigram, forms a holistic *gestalt*, as it addresses Billy's moments of engagement in the two narratives. In his second ekphrasis, Billy shows his engagement again through his activated fantasmic activity in an attempt to complete the narrative by means of mimetic coherence. That is, it demonstrates exactly what he wrote in his commentary: "I wanted to demonstrate my understanding of Nihad's reaction when he read the letter. The film and the book do not explain that." Billy pursues his fantasmic activity by explaining how relevant it is to know Nihad's point of view, and hypothesizes that perhaps he is not aware of his mother's death.

Billy's ekphrasis thus shows traces of engagement through the specific written moments. In the post-test, Billy's awareness of reactions had an incidence on flow

(Csikszentmihalyi, 1990), as he wrote: "I thought it was easy to do creative writing based on my reactions. Inspiration came to me naturally." Billy's concluding thoughts shed light on the usefulness of aesthetigrams in expanding on subjective responses to visual and written artworks. Billy's comment further illustrates that there is a way to help inspire students when they are asked to produce creative writing. There are solutions to the stifling phrase "Miss, I don't know what to write/where to start." Aesthetigrams allow for that type of self-investigation as inspiration for ekphrastic writing.

In his post-test, Billy offered additional feedback on aesthetigrams. He noted: "I think aesthetigrams helped me reflect on the play, especially on questions I would not have asked myself otherwise. They allowed me to craft my interpretation of the play." Such commentary speaks to Billy's previous statement on the type of contribution that aesthetigrams offer, specifically when it comes to fostering reflections and developing a critical eye on the reader's subjective interpretations. That is, rather than nurturing solipsism, aesthetigrams provide the visually attuned organization of one's perceived responses as they arise in one's consciousness. The mapping procedure gives participants a chance to show what they are capable of in terms of reading and viewing, fine-tuning their understandings, and meaning-making of narratives. In response to producing an aesthetigram for the visual narrative, Billy explained: "The aesthetigram I made for the movie helped me reflect on the story, it helped me understand the play better and compare the play and the film." The second mapping exercise thus shaped the participant's cognitive abilities through comparison of the visual and written narratives, helping him making sense of the written one and distinguishing its primary attributes from those of the multimodal narrative.

In a section where I asked participants to state whether they would replicate aesthetigram-making in academic circumstances, Billy thought it would be useful to make aesthetigrams in language courses again—this time in response to poetry: "It would be interesting to make aesthetigrams for poetry pieces because everybody reacts differently and poetry sparks a lot of emotions." Billy's comment towards the nature of the ideal texts for aesthetigram production is telling. In his view, creative writing, such as poetry, would lend itself well to interpretation through aesthetigrams.

Billy also expressed that he thought it would be useful to draw aesthetigrams for other movies in French classes and at home, especially classic films, popular films, film adaptations and cartoons. He expressed: "Movies sometimes spark more emotions in me than books because of their believability, so it would be more interesting making aesthetigrams in reaction to them."

My final comment on Billy's perceptions has to do with the fact that aesthetigrams, for the participant, should help uncover relationships with artworks that parallel real-life circumstances. In other words, using aesthetigrams as a way to map responses should guide readers in their explorations of narratives, insofar as they can help them clarify relationships between events and characters, and associations with plot intricacies. That is, aesthetigrams provide the highly sought-after opportunities to raise awareness of readers' capacities for shared human perceptions and feelings as components of reading engagement.

In summary, Billy's articulated definition of reading engagement informs ongoing developments and definitions of what it means to be engaged as an adolescent male reader. Among other detailed participant-generated definitions, I retained Billy's observations on reading engagement (shown in Chapter Four), which provide indicators valuing identification with characters, understanding and empathy with their storyline, and reading flow and pace. Billy's comparison between reading engagement and immersion in a TV show is telling in that regard. It further provides a concrete example of the meaning of being engaged, creating one's world (visual realization), not noticing time (reading-as-progression) and being immersed in it (judging characters and actions through axiological judgment, fantasmic activity, and mimetic coherence).

(Re)defining Reading Engagement: Visual Data Summarizing Key Points from the Larger Study

In this section, I provide a detailed picture of the responses that eleven boys from the larger study produced in response to the written play to grasp the affordances of aesthetigrams. These eleven students were chosen to showcase their diversity as readers and respondents.

I produced two charts from the data I analyzed. The first graph (Figure 20) offers a visual overview of the responses and emphases the participants identified in their aesthetigrams when reading scene 37 of *Incendies*. The second illustration (Figure 21) is a pie chart exemplifying the distribution of occurrences and percentages for each category of reaction as tracked in students' aesthetigrams.

In Figure 20, the reading engagement tendencies span over eleven categories. As such, Emotion and Reflection were the most selected categories in all aesthetigrams (82% of participants, or nine out of eleven participants). Taste was another popular category, as seven out of eleven participants used it in their map. Six students chose Perception and Explanation, while Feelings, Judgment, and Attitude were utilized by three boys. Finally, only two students marked their reactions in the Reverie and Knowledge/Content areas, and one student placed his responses in the Expectations category.

These response emphases point primarily to both the affective and reflective nature of students' reading encounters with the scene. These results are aligned with

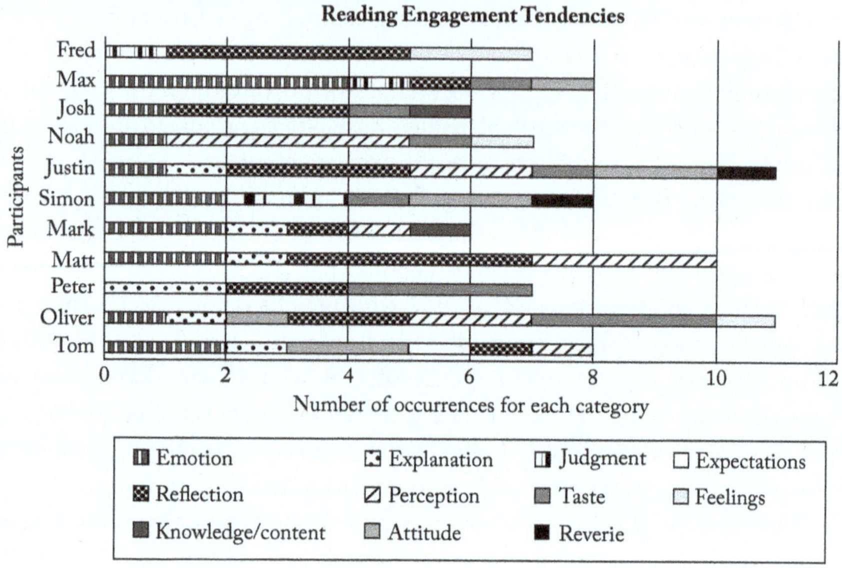

Figure 20: Reading engagement tendencies in participants.

the poignant essence of the textual narrative, and extend the varying and layered types of reading engagement that students experienced. It is telling that 82% of participants responded with both Emotion and Reflection, and such numbers provide evidence in the extrapolation of reading engagement's definition as it goes beyond simple meaning-making and comprehension strategies (Ivey & Johnston, 2013). Specifically, the Emotion category speaks to empathetic features of reading engagement (Muth, 2016; Sumara, Luce-Kapler & Iftody, 2008), while Reflection proposes avenues into higher cognitive engagement skills (Guthrie & Klauda, 2014). Conjointly, the popular Taste and Perception categories suggest inclinations towards the subjective nature of reading engagement, strengthening the purposeful need for alternative definitions of reading engagement (Ivey & Johnston, 2013).

As a category used to uncover the narrative's immanent "truths," the Explanation category is an extension of the Reflection category insofar as it triggers consideration of untangling plot events and characters' actions. These categories are also linked to Judgment, as a judgment response is the result of a reflection, depending on its intensity and duration.

Feelings and Attitude help readers name the unknown. On the one hand, the Feelings category allows participants to point to an emotion that is difficult to describe. On the other hand, the Attitude category aims to express arbitrary preferences without concrete justification. These response tendencies potentially point to male readers' capacity in this exercise to articulate properly, sometimes extensively, their responses to the written scene, even though these categories were less prominent in students' aesthetigrams.

I was surprised to see that a minority of students marked their responses in the Reverie area because, given readers' ability to experience narrative through imagined worlds, it could have given direct evidence to fictional empathy, for instance. Rather, indicators of reading engagement as identified through fictional empathy were marked as such in other categories like Judgment, Emotion, and Reflection.

Another less used category was Knowledge/Content, a more detached and objective orientation to the text. Context might have played an important role in determining these results. There is a possibility that not all students were familiar with the sociological and geographical concerns in the 1980's Middle East. However, the detachment that these students felt did not exclude them from identifying affective responses in their reception of the play. That is, a detachment response can overlap with an affective one at certain times, as readers engage with the narratives they read. To me it seems reasonable that this category was less used by participants because they were engaged through the other categories mentioned above. In terms of the number of times each category was used, the proportions differ slightly. Figure 21 provides a visual representation of the number of occurrences for each category used across all eleven participants. The following pie chart identifies these occurrences in detail:

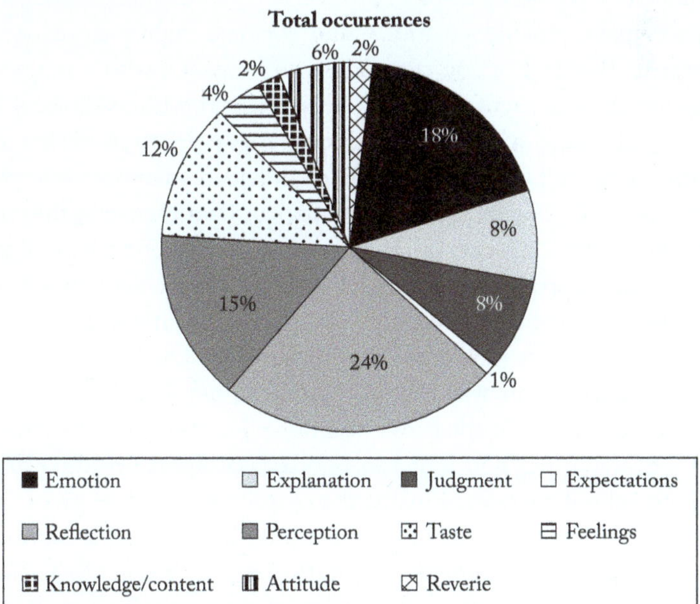

Figure 21: Total occurrences in reading tendencies.

In parallel with Figure 20, this pie chart reveals similar conclusions. The Emotion and Reflection dimensions are the categories with most appearances with respectively 24% and 18%. Perception comes third with 15%, closely followed by Taste with 12%. The categories that ensue are: Explanation (8%), Judgment (8%), Attitude (6%), Feelings (4%), Reverie (2%), Knowledge/Content (2%), and Expectations (1%).

The nature of the eleven participants' traces of engagement is, unsurprisingly, diverse. It spans over eleven categories, with Emotion and Reflection being the most popular categories, and Expectations being the least popular and used only once. That is, students' patterns of reading engagement were primarily emotionally and intellectually oriented, and not necessarily at the expense of one or the other. One of the main contributions of these results is that reading engagement traces, while different, can complement one another. Furthermore, this qualitative study provides specific insights into what it means to be an engaged reader in classroom contexts where students read narratives and watch its movie adaptation (with Julian's example).

Concluding Remarks

This case study depicted different layers of reading engagement and pointed to three major findings: (1) The comparisons between the two aesthetigrams, produced by the same participant, provide situational and concrete manifestations of the reader's engagement. That is, reaction categories can be coded with a range of indicators of engagement (e.g., reflections can be associated with axiological judgment, while moments identified with emotions or taste may point to awareness of aesthetic impact in the narrative); (2) These mappings provided snapshots into the reader's thought processes and experiences; response foci and patterns reflecting the reader's embedded values as he reads; and (3) The mapping process proved useful to promote learners' agency and meaning-making. The layers of engagement we see in the aesthetigrams give concrete traces of engagement that are identified with the indicators of engagement which were rooted in the literature on reading engagement.

Mapping reactions this way can help students develop their reading stances and develop an awareness of their own reactions. Furthermore, the study gives an example of a research method that can be used to observe reading engagement qualitatively in school contexts. Finally, the mapping procedure gives adolescents the agency and participatory readiness to communicate their transactional meaning-making. Aesthetigrams provide qualitative evidence regarding the range of types of reading engagement that adolescents can experience in reading and provide an alternative to the quantitative measures traditionally suggested by PISA.

Drifting away from crystallized guidelines of standardized testing to measure reading engagement, my hope is that these examples contribute to providing readers with a broader understanding of reading engagement.

References

Abram, D. (1997). *The spell of the sensuous: Perception and language in a more-than-human world.* New York, NY: Vintage Books.

Afonso, A. I. (2004). New graphics for old stories: Representation of local memories through drawings. In S. Pink, L. Kurti & A. I. Afonso (Eds.), *Working images: Visual research and representation in ethnography* (pp. 72–89). New York, NY: Routledge.

Barthes, R. (1973). *Le plaisir du texte.* Paris, France: Seuil.

Bogdan, D. (1992). *Re-education the imagination: Towards a poetics, politics, and pedagogy of literary engagement.* Portsmouth, NH: Heinemann.

Brehm, S. (2008). Le rôle de l'imaginaire dans le processus de référenciation. *Figura, 20,* 31–44.

Brehm, S. (2011). Du sens aux sens: Les représentations mentales dans l'acte de lecture. *Protée, 39*(2), 107–112.

Brehm, S. (2015). La lecture comme lieu de construction et d'appropriation d'un univers partagé. In M. Cambron & G. Langlade (Eds.). *L'événement de lecture* (pp. 231–248). Québec, QC: Nota Bene.

Brett, A. T. (2016). Seeking a balance: Discussion strategies that foster reading with authorial empathy. *Journal of Adult & Adolescent Literacy, 60*(3), 295–304.

Brozo, W. G. (2010). *To be a boy, to be a reader: Engaging teen and preteen boys in active literacy* (2nd ed.). Newark, DE: International Reading Association.

CMEC/Council of Ministers of Education, Canada. (2016). *Measuring up: Canadian results of the OECD PISA Study: The performance of Canada's youth in science, reading and mathematics. 2015 first results for Canadians aged 15.* Toronto, ON: Council of Ministers of Education, Canada.

Cremin, T. (2007). Revisiting reading for pleasure: Diversity, delight and desire. In K. Goouch & A. Lambirth (Eds.), *Understanding Phonics and the Teaching of Reading* (pp. 166–190). Berkshire, England: McGraw-Hill.

Cremin, T. (2014). Reading for pleasure and reader engagement: Reviewing the research. In T. Cremin, M. Mottram, S. Powell, R. Collins & K. Safford (Eds.), *Building Communities of Engaged Readers: Reading for pleasure* (pp. 5–19). London, England: Routledge.

Csikszentmihalyi, M. (1990). *Flow: The psychology of optimal experience.* San Francisco, CA: Harper Collins.

Ehret, C. (2018). Propositions from affect theory for feeling literacy through the event. In D. E. Alvermann, N. J. Unrau, M. Sailors & R. B. Ruddell (Eds.), *Theoretical models and processes of literacy* (pp. 563–580). New York, NY: Routledge.

Gervais, B. (1994/2006). *À l'écoute de la lecture.* Montréal, QC: Nota Bene.

Gervais, B. (1998). Progresser, comprendre : des régies de lecture. In C. Duchet & S. Vachon (Eds.), *La recherche littéraire : Objets et méthodes* (pp. 555–565). Montréal, QC : XYZ.

Guthrie, J. T. & Klauda, S. L. (2014). Effects of classroom practices on reading comprehension, engagement, and motivations for adolescents. *Reading Research Quarterly*, *49*(4), 387–416.

Hoffman, M.L. (2014). Empathy, social cognition and moral action. In W. M. Kurtines, J. Gewirtz & J. L. Lamb, *Handbook of Moral Behavior and Development* (vol. 1: Theory) (pp. 275–302). New York, NY: Psychology Press.

Ivey, G. & Johnson, P. H. (2013). Engagement with young adult literature: Outcomes and processes. *Reading Research Quarterly*, *48*(3), 255–275.

Jones, R. L. Jr. (1979). Phenomenological balance and aesthetic response. *Journal of Aesthetic Education*, *13*(1), 93–106.

Kendrick, M. & Rowsell, J. (2014). The visual turn: Transitioning into visual approaches to literacy education. In D. Jarvis & S. B. Elliott-John (Eds.), *Perspectives on transitions in schooling and instructional practice* (pp. 320–345). Toronto, ON: University of Toronto Press.

Klinger, D. A., Shulha, L. A. & Wade-Woolley, L. (2009). *Towards an understanding of gender differences in literacy achievement*. Toronto, ON: Government of Ontario, Education Quality and Accountability Office.

Lacelle, N. & Langlade, G. (2007). Former des lecteurs/spectateurs par la lecture subjective des œuvres. In J.-L. Dufays (Ed.), *Enseigner et apprendre la littérature aujourd'hui pour quoi faire?* (pp. 55–65). Louvain-la-Neuve, France: Presses Universitaires de Louvain.

Langlade, G. (2004). Sortir du formalisme, accueillir les lecteurs réels. *Le Français aujourd'hui*, 145, 85–96.

Langlade, G. (2006). L'activité fictionnalisante du lecteur. In M. Braud, B. Laville & B. Louichon (Eds.), *Les enseignements de la fiction* (pp. 163–176). Bordeaux, France: Presses de l'Université de Bordeaux.

Langlade, G. (2013). Chartreuse(s) de Parme: D'une lecture subjective à l'autre. In N. Rannou (Ed.). *L'expérience du sujet lecteur: travaux en cours* (pp. 41–53). Grenoble, France: Presses de l'Université de Grenoble.

Langlade, G. (2015). Événement de lecture et avènement du lecteur. In M. Cambron & G. Langlade (Eds.), *L'événement de lecture* (pp. 39–57). Québec, QC: Nota Bene.

Langlade, G. & Fourtanier, M.-J. (2007). La question du sujet lecteur en didactique de la lecture littéraire. In É. Falardeau, C. Fisher, C. Simard & N. Sorin (Eds.), *Didactique du français, les voies actuelles de la recherche* (pp. 101–123). Québec, QC: Les Presses de l'Université Laval.

Larrivé, V. (2015). Empathie fictionnelle et écriture en « je » fictif. *Repères*, 51, 157–176.

Lemieux, A. (2015). Think it through: Fostering aesthetic experiences to raise interest in literature at the high school level. *Journal of the Canadian Association for Curriculum Studies*, *12*(2), 66–93.

Lemieux, A. (2016). Moments de réception en lecture et en spectature : Le cas d'*Incendies* au CEGEP. *Revue de recherches en littératie médiatique multimodale (R2LMM)*, *3*(November, Special Issue, "Digital writing in schools: New textualities, new outcomes").

Lemieux, A. (2017). Recent developments: Aesthetigram-making in the literature classroom. In B. White & A. Lemieux (Eds.), *Mapping Holistic Learning: An introductory guide to aesthetigrams* (pp. 73–100). New York, NY: Peter Lang.

Lenters, K. (2016). Riding the lines and overwriting in the margins: Affect and multimodal literacy practices. *Journal of Literacy Research, 48*(3), 280–316.

Lewkowich, D. (2015). Transferences of teacher-casting and projections of redemptions: Teacher education, young adult literature and the psychic life of reading. *Pedagogy, Culture & Society, 23*(3), 349–368.

Lewkowich, D. (2016a). To enter the text as into a dream: Tracing the unconscious effects of reading experience. *International Journal of Research & Method in Education, 39*(1), 58–73.

Lewkowich, D. (2016b). The reader's read and the dreamer's dream: Fringing the unconscious. In G. Reis, A. Ibrahim & N. Ng-A-Fook (Eds.), *Provoking curriculum studies: Strong poetry and arts of the possible in education* (pp. 161–172). New York, NY: Routledge.

Lysaker, J. T. & Miller, A. (2012). Engaging social imagination: The developmental work of wordless book reading. *Journal of Early Childhood Literacy, 13*(2), 147–174.

Mitchell, C. (2011). *Doing visual research*. Thousand Oaks, CA: Sage.

Moss, G. (2007). *Literacy and gender: Researching texts, contexts and readers*. New York, NY: Routledge.

Moss, G. (2017). Assessment, accountability and the literacy curriculum: Reimagining the future in the light of the past. *Literacy, 51*(2), 56–64.

Muth, W. (2016). "A big circle of unity": Incarcerated fathers being-in-text. *Journal of Literacy Research, 48*(3), 317–345.

Nussbaum, M. C. (1998). *Cultivating humanity: A classical defense of reform in liberal education*. Cambridge, MA: Harvard University Press.

Pantaleo, S. (2013). Revisiting Rosenblatt's aesthetic response through *The Arrival*. *Australian Journal of Language and Literacy, 36*(3), 125–134.

People for Education/PfE. (2011). *Reading for joy*. Ontario Education Quality and Accountability Office (EQAO). Retrieved from http://www.peopleforeducation.ca/document/reading-for-joy

Ricoeur, P. (1981). *Hermeneutics and the human sciences: Essays on language, action and interpretation* (J. Thompson, Trans.). Cambridge, MA: Cambridge University Press, and Paris, France: Éditions de la Maison des Sciences de l'Homme.

Ricoeur, P. (1992). *Oneself as another*. Chicago, IL: Chicago University Press.

Rosenblatt, L. M. (1978). *The reader, the text, the poem: The transactional theory of the literary work*. Carbondale/Edwardsville: Southern Illinois University Press.

Rowsell, J. (2013). *Working with multimodality: Rethinking literacy in a digital age*. London, England: Routledge.

Rowsell, J. & Collier, D. (2016). Researching multimodality in language and education. In K. King, Y.-J. Lai & S. May (Eds.), *Encyclopedia of language and education* (pp. 1–14). Cham, Switzerland: Springer.

Rowsell, J. & Kendrick, M. (2013). Boys' hidden literacies: The critical need for the visual. *Journal of Adolescent and Adult Literacy, 56*(7), 587–599.

St. Clair, R. (2005). Similarity and superunknowns: An essay on the challenges of educational research. *Harvard Educational Review, 75*(4), 435–453.

Sumara, D. J. (2002). *Why reading literature in schools still matters: Imagination, interpretation, insight.* Mahwah, NJ: Lawrence Erlbaum.

Sumara, D., Luce-Kapler, R. & Iftody, T. (2008). Educating consciousness through literary experiences. *Educational Philosophy and Theory, 40*(1), 228–241.

Van Manen, M. (1990). *Researching lived experience: Human science for an action sensitive pedagogy.* London, ON: Althouse Press.

Van Manen, M. (2014). *Phenomenology of practice: Meaning-giving methods in phenomenological research and writing.* Walnut Creek, CA: Left Coast Press.

White, B. [Boyd]. (1998). Aesthetigrams: Mapping aesthetic experiences. *Studies in Art Education, 39*(40), 321–335.

White, B. [Boyd]. (2007). Aesthetic encounters: Contributions to teacher education. *International Journal of Education & the Arts, 8*(17), 1–28.

White, B. [Boyd]. (2011). Private perceptions, public reflections: Aesthetic encounters as vehicles for shared meaning making. *International Journal of Education & the Arts, 12*(LAI 2), 1–26.

White, B. [Boyd]. (2013). Pay attention, pay attention, pay attention. In B. White & T. Costantino (Eds.), *Aesthetics, empathy and education* (pp. 99–116). New York, NY: Peter Lang.

White, B. [Boyd]. (2014). Student generated art criticism. *Canadian Review of Art Education, 41*(1), 32–55.

White, B. [Boyd] & Lemieux, A. (2017). *Mapping holistic learning: An introductory guide to aesthetigrams.* New York, NY: Peter Lang.

White, B. [Boyd] & Tompkins, S. (2005). Doing aesthetics to facilitate meaning-making. *Arts and Learning Research Journal, 21*(1), 1–36.

White, B. [Bozena]. (2007). Are girls better readers than boys? Which boys? Which girls? *Canadian Journal of Education, 30*(2), 554–581.

CHAPTER FIVE

Community-Oriented Literacies and the Place of Materiality

Like many others who work in education and in related disciplines, I have always been fascinated by books. The title of this book suggests this continued, lifelong interest in printed materials (and digital ones as I discovered them later in life). In his chapter, I detail how a community literacy initiative I piloted at McGill University presented opportunities and challenges in offering and sharing printed books across a university campus. Specifically, I frame a proposition for sustainable literacy practices around considerations for material encounters, access, presence, mobility, and the place of materiality and new materialism in urban education.

Mobile Material Encounters and Objects of Fascination

Using visual literacy as an entrypoint to visual culture in education (Duncum, 2005; Heaton, 2014) and anthropological phenomenology as a fluctuating gaze on material culture (Ingold, 1995), I present the development of an idea that originated over the course of several walks in my old neighborhoods of Villeray and Mile-End-Parc-Extension; modest, family-oriented and student-infused neighborhoods located in Northern Montreal. The idea stemmed from the concept of a Little Free Library (LFL), a sustainable place for sharing books. I rely on Whatmore & Hinchliffe's (2018) proposition on "vernacular ecologies" (p. 450), whereby *citizens* determine community priorities, and are proactive in the shifts—cultural, material, ecological—they want to see. The shifts result from relationality and affectivity between more-than-humans and ecological environments, in which LFLs are human constructions taking place in naturalized environments. LFLs are places within those vernacular ecologies, with attention to space and place, and attuned to schools and parks as institutionalized establishments.

City wandering can lead to meaningful encounters with communities (Heng, 2018), and that is exactly what I experienced. The project stemmed from my wandering, several nights a week, where I would see LFLs throughout my neighborhood. It must be noted that I did not walk with researcher intentions—although one might argue that it is part of one's identity as a scholar, so I am still pondering that—but with the goal of unwinding and actually disconnecting from academic work. Cities are dynamic entities and pose compelling challenges for researchers (Lemieux & White, 2020; Knowles, 2018), but, of course, the context and grounding of those artifacts, and herein their pictures, determine interpretation (Bal, 2002) and thus the writing of this chapter. Not acknowledging those ramifications and repercussions would simply be dishonest and not rigorous.

Kathy Mills (2016) described how engaging in literacy practices and events calls for an acute self-awareness of the senses, especially when doing "sensory walks with a camera" (p. 138). While walking in my neighborhood, I did not bring my DSLR camera, but my iPhone gave me the affordance of capturing the images of the LFLs, all the while being in the moment. Mobile technologies allow for these types of literacies-in-the-moment (MacEntee, Burkholder & Schwab-Cartas, 2016; Nordquist, 2017). The following pictures are thus framed with my own perceptions of what literacy is, and so these perceptions necessarily "come from somewhere" (Patoine, 2015, p. 64), and therefore cannot escape power structures. And because perceptions are simulations, some aesthetic attention focuses on what is (and what is not) sensed beyond the biological and includes the relational.

Little did I know that the action of *choosing to take a photograph* as a hobby—or even just to remember the novelty of the idea—was, as Sontag (1973) described, encountering "an object of fascination" (p. 17), for "each still photograph is a privileged moment, turned into a slim object that one can keep and look at again" (Sontag, 1973, p. 22), whether those pictures are material, digital, or hybrid.

And so, the act of going through my iPhone pictures, reminiscing about that material encounter with LFLs, developed into a funded project that has now expanded to 18 locations across the McGill campus, thanks to the efforts of collaborators Elena Bouton, Merika Ramundo, the Sustainability Office, and the McGill Library. Both the Sustainability Office and the McGill Library saw in this idea a potential for literacy sustainability—revitalizing printed books in a digital

Figure 22: Community-based LFL in Rosemont, picture taken by Lemieux with an iPhone 5, 2015.

era, establishing a community-oriented initiative, and promoting literacy in higher education. A pilot LFL was made from recycled materials such as a wooden stool, old nails, a wooden box, and some pre-owned paint. Launched in January 2016, the project was well received in the Faculty of Education and made waves beyond the department walls[9]. "The power of literacy," Orellana (2017) writes, "is not just that it allows words and ideas to travel across time and space and to move across borders that sometimes keep people out. It is that words can travel between minds and hearts" (p. xviii).

On the heels of the success of the pilot, I submitted a follow-up proposal to the Sustainability Office that was titled "Sustainable Literacy at McGill University: The Little Free Libraries (LFLs) Project" as a participatory solution to the abundance of books left or forgotten in faculty hallways and student areas.

9. For more detail on the pilot project, please see Lemieux and McLarnon (2018).

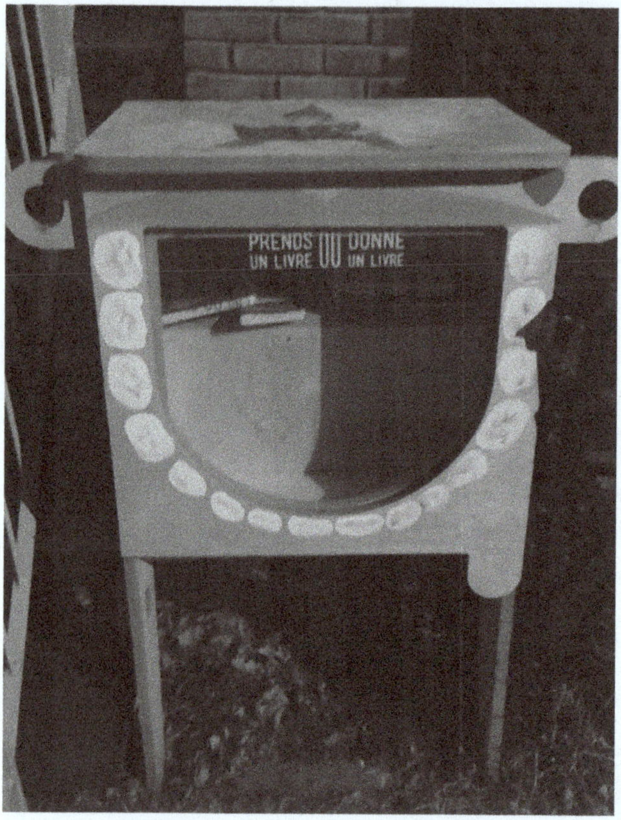

Figure 23: Community-based LFL in Villeray, Montreal, picture taken by Lemieux with an iPhone 5, 2015.

Seeking to expand this project to McGill community members across campus, I reached out to Merika Ramundo and this initiative developed into a joint proposal funded by the McGill Library Innovation Fund. The now larger project sought to address the goals of the McGill 2020 Vision Plan: sustainability, diversity, equity, education, and lifelong learning in higher education and beyond. As explained elsewhere, this LFL initiative bolstered communal democratic engagement simply by its presence and its accessibility to most people on campus and with the aims of serving the public good (Lemieux & McLarnon, 2018).

Now let's take a closer look at Figure 24. The library hub, tangible and palpable in real life (going to these campus locations, feeling, hearing, touching, browsing), only permeates the text through the image here, actualizing itself through visual cues, marking its own local *différenciation* in the process, actualizing it as a reality taking place (Deleuze, 1968). As with any valid and thorough visual analysis, my commentary here benefits from going beyond mere description (Pink, 2004), and

Figure 24: LFL Pilot, © Lemieux, picture taken with an iPhone 5.

by connecting theory with praxis. As I think with theory now, and as I have suggested in Chapter One, this picture is situated in place and time, and looking back at it and comparing it to its later developments will, hopefully, guide the reader in the transformative process that went on in this project.

Access, Space, and Place

Community engagement, knowledge sharing through creative spaces, inclusivity, and accessibility were main objectives of the original LFL proposal. A second phase of the project developed into a larger community-wide initiative taken over by institutional university units. In later readings, it made sense that democratizing education happens through maker mindsets (Halverson & Sheridan, 2014; Peppler & Bender, 2013) in the same ways that making and crafting artifacts can be done with sustainable purposes and aims in mind. Thinking with posthuman phenomenology (Neimanis, 2018), with a call for "our embodiment and becoming-with other bodies evidences an inescapable co-constitution of nature and culture, of imagination and matter" (p. 64), it makes sense that the interweaving of crafting for the public good, for public literacy access in this case, is made holistically and organically. Therefore, I determined the locations of the first five LFLs in accordance with what I ethnographically observed as faculties where there were (1) oftentimes books left in hallways, and considering (2) the number of university community members who regularly walked by those locations. I identified the Faculty of Arts, the Leacock building, the Student Centre, the Burnside building, and the McGill library as accessible and high flux passage locations. While one could think that locations 2 (Leacock) and 3 (Arts) are close to each other, the

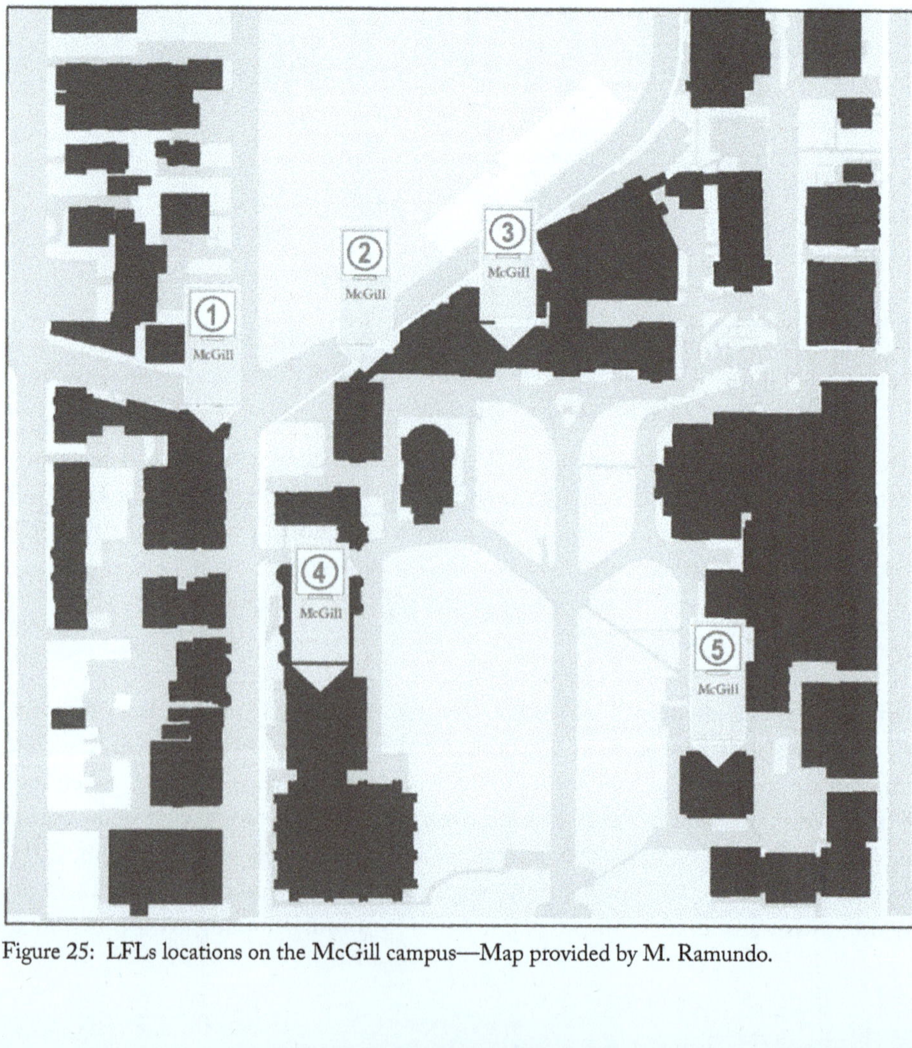

Figure 25: LFLs locations on the McGill campus—Map provided by M. Ramundo.

number of people who pass by these locations is extensive and they also come from different disciplines. The East side of campus benefits from the presence of a LFL in Burnside, and more locations have been added since as part of the developments made by the McGill Library.

Presence, Mobility, Wanderings: Reflections on Materiality

Like in Chapter One, in which I presented a walk-through of Montreal and an ekphrastic poetry piece as a relational rendering of feeling and being in the moment, I reflect on how material agency "allows us to focus upon the way in which people and things are mutually related" (Jones & Boivin, 2018, pp. 350–351). With the Little Free Library Project, I had not anticipated the scope this idea would take over a three year span, and how connected I would feel to both tangible and intangible community-objects (I hyphenize the latter, for the relational speaks to the project as entity and its ripple effects beyond the "place" of the campus). Looking back

Figure 26: Faculty of Arts LFL (location #3), picture provided by M. Ramundo.

across the different phases, it has become clear that I framed those original pictures as ideas visually materialized, as "photo-elicitations" (Pink, 2004, p. 2). That is, the photographs present what is and what is not there. People were not there, only books and their potential for outreach. Looking back at my photo essay in Chapter One, the same thinking could be applied. I took the pictures with my DSLR camera, but my gaze was not towards people; it was towards atmosphere, lighting, emotion... what was there and what could not be grasped through a snapshot. Photography allows one to capture those atmospheres, fleeting moments and lightings, similarly to the aesthetigrams found in Chapters Two and Three on reading engagement. Because behind the snapshots lie humans, more-than-humans, 'superunknowns,' doubts, fears, heartbreaks, breakups, an infinite myriad of things that are palpable and things that are yet to be. Education's focus is to get at least to glimpses of that complexity, as to permeate the essence of teaching and learning.

When it comes to the role of books in education, printed books embody materiality in ways that are embedded in time. Historically, books have been part of school materialities (Depaepe, Simon & Verstraete, 2014) and universities are no exception, even to this day. Despite the shift to eBooks and journal subscriptions in recent (and future) years, meaning and meaning-making extend the life books and sign language (Stahl, 2018), and seek, in their own way, to get at the snapshots that I have described just now. Dynamism between printed books and humans as living libraries themselves allows for a constant flux between crafted objects as library hubs, sharing intent, and the epistemological and ideological effects of books on humans themselves. As "micro-urban interventions" (Sarmiento, Sims & Morales, 2018), Little Free Libraries connect material, humans, more-than-humans, spaces, places, ideas, and histories in plural *timespacematterings* (Barad, 2007). As with agential cuts (Barad, 2007), performativity defines agency as a matter of intra-acting; it happens in relationality and is not bound by, or does not belong to, humans/subjects.

But my gaze, as researcher-photographer, cannot be subdued and arguing otherwise would be fallacy. How can writing—and especially research writing—be devoid of the very lens it requires to produce ideas and materialize them through images, graphs, and signifiers? I still reflect on that question daily. Language is privileged over matter in research, but with alternative perspectives and epistemologies, it is my hope that we can bend research traditions and consider posthuman-centric methods. Schadler (2017) has done work towards debunking these traditions, rooting for the intricate relationships between new ways of doing ethnography with posthumanist concerns as work within the self (autoethnography), duoethnography, maker and artifact work, and collaborations with community members and artists. As Schadler (2017) maintains: "To disseminate my research in articles or presentations, I rebuild worlds in written words or visual data. These presentations are not considered a representation of the research object; rather, they are the research outcome and its intracontextual processes in its current form of becoming" (p. 512). The contents presented in this book are intrinsically linked to the environments in which they became, and in which they evolved over time. What is more, "Literacies in community contexts are nested within the cultural, economic, and social forces that surround them" (Rowsell et al., 2019, p. 524). The writing, as a post-encounter and a post-reflective activity, speaks to my own relationality, the relational effects of objects on each other, and on my own research process. Intuitive practice, among others, proves to be another method that allows for pragmatism and materialist engagement with local and global environments (De Freitas & Ferrara, 2016).

Closing, Looking Beyond, Looking Ahead

This book has invited multiple reflections on phenomenology and posthumanism as they relate to language, literacy practices, and reading engagement. I have argued that researcher positionality can shift depending on what is researched, inquired, or studied, but the epistemologies I surveyed corroborate each other, overlap, flirt and sometimes disagree with each other. To exemplify this, and for the time being, I rely on Neimanis's (2018) position on posthumanism, reminding us that:

> A posthuman phenomenology also reminds posthumanists that the embeddedness of bodies within contexts, with specific possibilities and matrices of power, cannot be transcended. A posthuman method can no more easily escape the situatedness of the practitioner than a phenomenological one can. (p. 64)

Abram (1997) also explained that literacy should be understood in relation to "the multiple nonhuman shapes and powers that lend their influence to all our activities," (p. 123) and that those activities—implying 'our'—are human in this case. As Dernikos, Ferguson & Siegel (2019) point out, the ethical "doing" of posthumanism is a lot messier in practice, and researchers as humans are always haunted by the ghosts of humanism, which has both positive and negative repercussions. Data takes a more-than-human dimension and, therefore, breeds on an "afterlife" (Dernikos, Ferguson & Siegel, 2019). Synesthetic human-object experiences are still at the core of literacy development, for language still constitutes, to this day, the primary mode through which we share research internationally. However, sensory synesthetic experiences between self↔environment allows for the environment to become part of the self, and to the self to become part of the environment, holistically. The human capacity to see itself as one with materials is a realization and move towards the end of subject-object dichotomies. If literacy researchers and practitioners continue their efforts to erase those dichotomies, the focus on standardized testing and "readiciding" (Gallagher, 2009) texts and the classroom, too, will fade.

Final Walk

During the 2018 United Kingdom Literacy Association Conference in Cardiff, Wales, I wandered through the streets and ventured to Cardiff Bay. Like any scholar who travels, I had my iPhone with me to browse through the schedule before the conference and decide on my agenda, people to meet, and talks to attend. I was embracing my *flâneuse* role—where I engaged my sense with my surroundings through an impromptu walk (Dobson, 2018)—before engaging in what was to be intense academic work. Looking at Dobson's (2018) four urban pedagogy assertions (flâneur/se→educating the senses→the influence of signs/codes→commodity) reminds us that making and building community projects with the aim of working towards better literacy futures is linked to urban experiences and social (re)codings of places and spaces, notably to foster a sense of belonging and extend literacy repertoires (Comber, 2015). The Little Free Library Project certainly was designed for this purpose and had similar outcomes. That is, sustainability and material literacy initiatives have the power to transform landscapes, generate new ideas, and build community bonds that are necessary for collaboration, cooperation, and altruism in education and beyond.

In closing, I walk you through the lens I used to capture glimpses of urban literacies, where I saw a crocodile vamping on the Cardiff Bay sand in the summer of 2018. I had no researcher intent, but, similar to my experience in Northern Montreal, I wonder whether I can separate that gaze from even the most mundane activities. As I walked, I noticed the book *The Enormous Crocodile* was cracked opened and served as a bench on which people could sit. It took me a few seconds to get that the crocodile was the main character who escaped from the book, materializing as part of the real-world landscape. In consideration for the repercussions of materiality on human thought, Sameshima, White & Sinner (2019) adapted the Japanese theory of 'MA' to material culture and curriculum studies, as a metaphor to examine the distance and spaces between humans and materiality. These spaces, Sameshima (2019) explains, need to be understood more fully in such investigations of curriculum practices:

> The body itself is the mediator; and thus the artifacts I make, extensions of me, instigate meaning. If I imagine MA as the interval between two markers—if one marker

> is data and the other is understanding—the stepping stones that allow the body to move across, draw connection, or close distance between the two markers, are the constructed artifacts. The material objects allow traversal across and through *what once was an unnamed or unattended void*. (p. 8, my emphasis)

I emphasize here the "once unnamed" and the "unattended void," which recalls the original Little Free Library idea that emerged from a street walk to a campus-wide funded project. Literacy is considered 'holistic' when it broaches the idea of being able to acknowledge its material presence and engage with its aesthetic, cognitive, spatial, and visual components as part of the perceptive self. In the case of the LFLs, willful subjects become one with the objects they desire—me, for example, walking through Montreal neighborhoods or by the Cardiff seaside towards the crocodile and the book from which it resurfaced—and ekphrasis can allow bolstering relational literacies development from these material encounters. And so in closing, I leave you with an ekphastic poetry piece I crafted from a post-encounter with these two photographs. It is my hope that this process can be replicated or adapted for engagement purposes, either for yourself as researcher, or in your classroom if you are a practitioner.

Figure 27: Cardiff, taken with iPhone 8, 2018.

Figure 28: Cardiff, taken with iPhone 8, 2018.

6,000 kilometres from Montreal to Cardiff,
Similar propositions, like-minded concerns
With a purpose that is stern
Rising above the cliff
Crocodile forging his traces on the sand
Croc in the dock they say, Cardiff Bay
Reminiscing the feel of my brown leather shoes
tapping the historic sidewalk flagstones
towards fragments of them as
dunes of sand upon which is rested
A cracked open book
Sit on these words,
See how they feel, Feel how they see
By the sea
A soul with a view
Engulfed in the sun's energy going a distance
Sunglasses needed, will keep those words to myself
As beams glean on the pages,
Waves hitting the shore like commas rhythming phrases
Between two phases,
The enormous crocodile has also walked on these old slabs
Since 1978

Marked children, youth, adults, laughs, sounds, picture,
Still in the picture, green presence on blue landscape
Stiff as a layout margin from the very book it took life from,
Tail curved like an apostrophe pulling the waves in
The coastal shore of this instant in which
The croc, versatile as a reptile of his own,
awaits minds like mine
who wander on the beach
sea salt taste on my lips
and wonder about the words that materialized
over time, its very presence as a matter of souls living together
rather than minds bound by language.

Acknowledgements

For this chapter, the author would like to acknowledge the funding awarded by the McGill Sustainability Office and the McGill Library Innovation Fund, and thank Merika Ramundo, Communications Officer at McGill University, who provided the pictures for the larger LFL project. The larger project and its ongoing state would not have been possible without her leadership. Many thanks to Elena Bouton from University of California-Berkeley College of Environmental Design and Architecture, as she was part of one of the most integral parts of the project and its development in the mid-stages. Thank you to Mitchell McLarnon for his work on the pilot stage. The author acknowledges the editorial *rigueur* of Emily MacKinnon and her fine balance between kindness and diligence in the process. Finally, thank you to Marie-France Guénette for, well, everything.

References

Abram, D. (1997). *The spell of the sensuous: Perception and language in a more-than-human world.* New York, NY: Vintage Books.

Bal, M. (2002). *Travelling concepts in the humanities.* Toronto, ON: University of Toronto Press.

Barad, K. (2007). *Meeting the universe halfway: Quantum physics and the entanglement of matter and meaning.* Durham, NC/London, England: Duke University Press.

Comber, B. (2015). *Literacy, place, and pedagogies of possibility.* New York, NY: Routledge.

De Freitas, E. & Ferrara, F. (2016). Matter, movement, and memory. In N. Snaza, D. Sonu, S. E. Truman & Z. Zaliwska (Eds.), *Pedagogical matters: New materialisms and curriculum studies* (pp. 43–57). New York, NY: Peter Lang.

Deleuze, G. (1968). *Différence et répétition.* Paris, France: Presses universitaires de France.

Depaepe, M., Simon, F. & Verstraete, P. (2014). Valorising the cultural heritage of the school desk through historical research. In P. Smeyers & M. Depaepe (Eds.), *Educational Research: Material Culture and its Representation* (pp. 13–30). Cham, Switzerland: Springer.

Dernikos, B. P., Ferguson, D. & Siegel, M. (2019). The possibilities for "humanizing" posthumanist inquiries: An intra-active conversation. *Cultural Studies ↔ Critical Methodologies*, 1–14. DOI:10.1177/1532708619829793.

Dobson, S. (2018). Urban pedagogy and the need to develop city skills. In S. Nichols & S. Dobson (Eds.), *Learning cities: Multimodal explorations and placed pedagogies* (pp. 111–129). Singapore: Springer.

Duncum, P. (2005). Visual culture art education: Why, what and how. In R. Hickman (Ed.), *Critical Studies in Art & Design Education* (pp. 151–162). Bristol, England/Portland, ME: Intellect.

Gallagher, K. (2009). *Readicide: How schools are killing reading and what you can do about it.* Portland, ME: Stenhouse.

Halverson, E. R. & Sheridan, K. (2014). The maker movement in education. *Harvard Educational Review, 84*(4), 495–504.

Heaton, R. (2014). Moving mindsets: Re-conceptualising the place of visual culture as multi-sensory culture in primary education. *Canadian Review of Art Education, 41*(1), 77–96.

Heng, T. (2018). Walking through spiritual neighbourhoods: A photo essay. In S. Nichols & S. Dobson (Eds.), *Learning cities: Multimodal explorations and placed pedagogies* (pp. 95–107). Singapore: Springer.

Ingold, T. (1995). Building, dwelling, living—How animals and humans make themselves at home in the world. In M. Starthern (Ed.), *Shifting contexts: Transformations in anthropological knowledge* (pp. 57–80). London, England: Routledge.

Jones, A. M. & Boivin, N. (2018). The malice of inanimate objects: Material agency. In D. Hicks & M. C. Beaudry, *The Oxford Handbook of Material Culture Studies* (pp. 333–351). Oxford, England: Oxford University Press.

Knowles, C. (2018). Researching and photographing cities: Getting started. In S. Nichols & S. Dobson (Eds.), *Learning cities: Multimodal explorations and placed pedagogies* (pp. 9–21). Singapore: Springer.

Lemieux, A. & McLarnon, M. (2018). Artful portable library spaces: Increasing community agency and shared knowledge. In E. Hasebe-Ludt & C. Leggo (Eds.), *Canadian Curriculum Studies: A Métissage of Inspiration/Imagination/Interconnection* (pp. 35–46). Toronto, ON: Canadian Scholars' Press.

Lemieux, A. & White, B. (2020). Walking with Wonder: Attunement to the senses and relationality in photographic inquiry. In H. Mreweid, M.C. Carter & C. Mitchell (Eds.), *Art as an Agent for Social Change*. Boston, MA: Brill-Sense.

MacEntee, K., Burkholder, C. & Schwab-Cartas, J. (Eds.). (2016). *What's a cellphilm?: Integrating mobile phone technology into participatory visual research and activism.* Rotterdam, Netherlands: Sense Publishers.

Mills, K. A. (2016). *Literacy theories for the digital age: Social, critical, multimodal, spatial, material and sensory lenses.* Bristol, England: Multilingual Matters.

Neimanis, A. (2018). Posthuman phenomenologies for planetary bodies of water. In C. Åsberg & R. Braidotti (Eds.), *A feminist companion to the posthumanities* (pp. 55–66). Cham, Switzerland: Springer Nature.

Nordquist, B. (2017). *Literacy and mobility.* New York, NY: Routledge.

Orellana, M. F. (2017). Foreword. In R. Zaidi & J. Rowsell (Eds.), *Literacy Lives in Transcultural Times* (pp. viii–x). New York, NY: Routledge.

Patoine, P.-L. (2015). *Corps/Texte—Pour une théorie de la lecture empathique : Cooper, Danielewski, Frey, Palahniuk.* Lyon, France: École Normale Supérieure Éditions.

Peppler, K. & Bender, S. (2013). Spreading innovation: Leveraging lessons from the maker movement. *Phi Delta Kappan, 95*(3), 22–27.

Pink, S. (2004). Introduction: Situating visual research. In S. Pink, L. Kürti & A. I. Afonso (Eds.), *Working images: Visual research and representation in ethnography* (pp. 1–12). London, England: Routledge.

Rowsell, J., Kress, G., Pahl, K. & Street, B. V. (2019). The social practice of multimodal reading: A New Literacy Studies-Multimodal perspective on reading. In D. E. Alvermann, N. J. Unrau, M. Sailors & R. B. Ruddell (Eds.), *Theoretical models and processes of literacy* (pp. 514–532). New York, NY: Routledge.

Sameshima, P. (2019). Ma, I'm thinking about nothing. In P. Sameshima, B. White & A. Sinner (Eds.), *Ma: Materiality in teaching and Learning.* New York, NY: Peter Lang.

Sameshima, P., White, B. & Sinner, A. (2019). *Ma: Materiality in teaching and learning.* New York, NY: Peter Lang.

Sarmiento, C. S., Sims, R. J. & Morales, A. (2018). Little free libraries: An examination of micro-urbanist interventions. *Journal of Urbanism: International Research on Placemaking and Urban Sustainability, 11*(2), 233–253.

Schadler, C. (2017). How to define situated and ever-transforming family configurations? A new materialist approach. *Journal of Family Theory & Review, 8*, 503–514.

Sontag, S. (1973/2005). *On photography.* New York, NY: Rosetta Books.

Stahl, A.B. (2010/2018). Material histories. In D. Hicks & M.C. Beaudry. *The Oxford Handbook of Material Culture Studies* (pp. 150–172). Oxford: Oxford University Press.

White, B. & Lemieux, A. (2015). Reflecting selves: Pre-service teacher identity development explored through material culture. *LEARNing Landscapes, 9*(1), 267–283.

Whitmore, S. & Hinchliffe, S. (2018). Ecological landscapes. In D. Hicks & M. C. Beaudry (Eds.), *The Oxford handbook of material culture studies* (pp. 440–458). Oxford, England: Oxford University Press.

Index

A

B

C

D

E

K

L

M

N

O

P

R

W

Y

Z